Sleeping with Rhinos

JOURNEYS TO WILD PLACES

Robin and Arlene Karpan

PARKLAND
PUBLISHING

Saskatoon

Published in Canada in 2013 by
Parkland Publishing
501 Mount Allison Place
Saskatoon, Saskatchewan
Canada S7H 4A9

Telephone: 306-242-7731
info@parklandpublishing.com
www.parklandpublishing.com

Printed in Canada by Houghton Boston, Saskatoon.

Parkland Publishing acknowledges the support of the Creative Industry Growth and Sustainability program made possible through funding provided to the Saskatchewan Arts Board by the Government of Saskatchewan through the Ministry of Tourism, Parks, Culture, and Sport.

Library and Archives Canada Cataloguing in Publication
Karpan, Robin, author
Sleeping with rhinos : journeys to wild places / Robin and Arlene Karpan.
ISBN 978-0-9809419-4-4 (pbk.)
1. Karpan, Robin--Travel. 2. Karpan, Arlene--Travel.
3. Adventure travel. 4. Voyages around the world.
I. Karpan, Arlene, author II. Title.
G439.K36 2013 910.4'1 C2013-905639-4

Front cover: *White rhinoceros, South Africa.*

CONTENTS

Introduction

This book originated from the sheer joy of travel. We have wandered around some exciting parts of the globe over the years, both in our work as travel writers and photographers, and as ordinary travellers simply curious to see what lies over the next hill. As much as we've enjoyed the attractions of great cities and great civilizations, what has stayed with us the most are the wonders of nature – breathtaking landscapes, unspoiled wilderness, fascinating wildlife. The more we travel these days, the more we're drawn to those exceptional places. Unfortunately, these parts of the world are disappearing the fastest.

The world continues to change, as it always has, although today we seem to be living in an era of unprecedented transformation, both good and bad. When it comes to the natural world, the news tends to be more bad than good – population pressures, global warming, deforestation, more species becoming extinct. A month before publication, news reports raised concerns that after an unusually low migration of monarch butterflies to Mexico, parts of Canada that usually have plenty of returning monarchs have none at all. Only time will tell if this is a temporary glitch or something more serious. There is less question about the seriousness of the rhino poaching problem in South Africa, or the impact of global warming on the Arctic. UNESCO may revoke World Heritage Site status from Ethiopia's Simien Mountains if human impact continues to be a problem. Closer to home, we've watched dramatic changes over a couple of decades as loggers, miners, and road builders penetrate deeper into pristine boreal forest, lakelands, and river valleys of the northern Saskatchewan wilderness.

While there is much to lament, this collection of stories celebrates the joys of discovering nature's wonders – the thrill of getting close to Africa's great predators, watching the sun rise from atop a giant sand dune in the Namibian desert, gazing over the stark beauty of Antarctica, rambling through the wilds of Patagonia. If the world's special places and special creatures are to survive, it will be because people know about them and care about them.

These stories span several years, and range from the Arctic to Antarctic, Africa to Latin America, to a tiny spec in the middle of the Pacific Ocean. Above all, *Sleeping with Rhinos* is an escape from our increasingly over-crowded, over-urbanized, and over-civilized world to places where wildness is valued and Mother Nature still has some clout.

Trekking on the Roof of Africa
Ethiopia's Simien Mountains

Trekking guide Getachew in the Simien Mountains.

Our lungs gasp for air with each upward step. The air thins as our path tops altitudes over 4,000 metres, but jaw-dropping views more than make up for the discomfort. Standing on the edge of the escarpment, we gaze in awe over soaring jagged peaks, stone columns, and gorges dropping into oblivion. Not only does this dramatic land hold some of the most impressive landscapes anywhere, it's home to plants and animals found nowhere else on Earth.

The Simien Mountains of northern Ethiopia are known as the Roof of Africa. While a few other African peaks are higher, Mount

Kilimanjaro being the most famous, they are mostly individual mountains. The Simiens are part of a vast mountain plateau with several peaks topping 4,000 metres; Ras Dashen is the highest, at 4,543 metres. This combination of outstanding scenery and habitat for rare species earned the Simien Mountains UNESCO World Heritage Site status. Indeed, it was among the original 12 places in the world so named in 1978 when the United Nations first started designating sites of outstanding cultural or natural significance.

We start our journey with a one-hour flight from the Ethiopian capital of Addis Ababa to the northern city of Gonder, a former ancient capital dominated by a 17th century castle, also a World Heritage Site. Dubbed the Camelot of Africa, the fairly-tale castle built by Emperor Fasil is part of a rambling walled Royal Enclosure filled with palaces, churches, banquet halls, and even a cage that held lions.

Gonder brims with history at every turn. We wander through the ornate Debre Birhan Selasie Church, dating to 1690, where colourful Biblical scenes cover every inch of the interior. The life of Christ is portrayed, St. George is slaying the dragon, and a fearsome painting of the Devil surrounded by flames reminds the faithful not to stray. The ceiling is adorned with the faces of 80 winged cherubs, each with a different expression.

Christianity was embraced in Ethiopia even before Europe. The enduring history and traditions of the Ethiopian Orthodox Church continue to pervade the life of the country. The day we arrive, crowds are gathering in the streets outside our hotel. A funeral procession is underway for a high ranking priest, with chanting and ceremony at several stops along the slow route to the church. The funeral is somber but certainly not drab. Many wear robes of pure white, while some priests and attendants are dressed to the hilt in a rainbow of colours, carrying umbrellas in dazzling shades of red and gold.

Our main purpose in coming to Gonder is to visit the Simien Mountains. While we have a general idea of what we want to do, we arrive without concrete plans. It takes surprisingly little time to make arrangements. It's a fair bet that any foreigners wandering around Gonder are likely heading to the mountains, so they soon catch the eye of trekking organizers. Our hotel arranges for one such organizer, Abiyot Admassu, to come to talk to us. Before long, we work out a five-day hiking and camping trip. It seems like there is a lot to put together: transport to the park, a guide, cook, food, camping gear, and mules with handlers to carry gear between camps.

"No problem," says Abiyot. "If I know before 2:00 pm, we can be ready to leave first thing tomorrow morning."

Early next morning we're off on the three-hour trip by van to Debark, home to the national park headquarters. The drive is an eye-opening introduction to rural Ethiopia, with people literally everywhere. With around 90 million inhabitants, Ethiopia is the second most populous country in Africa, after Nigeria. Cities such as Addis Ababa teem with people, but urban areas are a mere drop in the bucket. Over 90 per cent of the population is rural, with most people eking out a subsistence living.

It's well into the dry season during our February visit. Hills and fields are brown and bone dry, as they are expected to be at this time. Most crops have been harvested, with straw stacks dotting the landscape. Only a few stands of barley, the crop of choice in much of this region, await cutting. Plots of land vary in size, but most are tiny, some less than an acre. Large fields are not necessary when most farming is done by hand or with animals.

To much of the world, the mere mention of Ethiopia evokes stark images of the 1980s famine. The northern part of the country was especially hard hit by severe drought, made all the worse by mismanagement and corruption by the extremist Marxist government, and civil war as Eritrea fought for independence from Ethiopia. Historians still debate how much of the famine was caused by drought and how much by politics. Ethiopians today are anxious to shed that pervasive, stereotypical image, although the country remains among the poorest nations on Earth. Travelling through the parched land, it's easy to see how things could deteriorate so quickly. Many people just scrape by at the best of times. If the rains don't come when expected, consequences are serious.

Traffic on the highway is fairly light – motorized traffic that is. There's no shortage of donkey carts, herds of sheep and goats, horses, mules, and people walking. Passing through villages, we have to negotiate the mass of humanity and livestock that usually spills onto the road. The van driver leans on the horn and the mass slowly parts enough for us to make it through. We hit a traffic jam behind a slow-moving donkey cart, its driver wrapped in a blanket that covers his head like a hood. The rickety cart is hauling a load of firewood, its wheels wobbling as if they're about to fall off. The scene seems right out of Biblical times, except that the driver is talking on his cell phone. It never ceases to amaze us how remote places in one of the poorest countries in the world could have better cell service than we have in many rural areas where we live.

In early morning, kids are on their way to school. Most are walking, but we see a surprising number running along the side of the highway that winds through the hilly countryside. Walking is normal for most students, but if they live a long way from school, they may run part of the way. Ethiopia is famous for its marathon and long distance runners, many excelling in Olympic competitions. Abiyot tells us that this is how many top athletes got their start, running for a very practical reason – it's a long way to school. No worries about childhood obesity here.

Debark is a crowded dusty town, made all the more chaotic because the highway through town is being rebuilt, and we've arrived on market day. We stop to register at the national park office, where Abiyot turns us over to Getachew, our guide, and Jemale, a scout with the national park. Park regulations stipulate that every party heading into the mountains has to be accompanied by an armed scout for protection. Protection from what isn't all that clear. Bandits roamed the hills many years ago, but these days hiring a scout is more about providing employment in this impoverished region than the need for protection. Never without the Kalashnikov rifle slung over his shoulder, Jemale turns out to be an amiable hiking companion.

To leave Debark, our van weaves through the central market, now bursting with people and their wares. Winding up the dusty hills on the outskirts of town, we travel headlong into a steady stream of people, carts, and livestock flooding toward the market. Many people lug heavy loads, while others carry only a couple long eucalyptus poles that they hope to sell for building material.

Higher and higher we climb into the mountains, enter the national park gates, and before long are dropped off with Getachew and Jemale for a four-hour hike to the first campsite. The relatively short walk helps us acclimatize to high altitudes, with little altitude gain as we follow the edge of the escarpment. Since we are already at over 3,200 metres, we are treated to stunning views right from the start. It's difficult to imagine a more formidable terrain. Remnants of ancient volcanoes and 40 million years of erosion have formed a sea of barbed peaks and pinnacle rocks, broken by gorges and chasms. Some cliff faces drop over a kilometre, almost straight down.

The mountains are known for their high biodiversity, including several endemic plants and animals. Even in the dry season, assorted flowering plants cover the land. Wild thyme is abundant, its pink-purple flowers carpeting the ground and emitting a pleasant fragrance as we walk through meadows. We see plenty of Abyssinian rose, white-blossomed plants reaching three metres or more, the only rose native to Africa. Most impressive are giant lobelias, short palm trees with long flower stems that shoot straight up as much as 10 metres.

In late afternoon we arrive at Sankaber campsite, nestled in a clump of trees near a spectacular clifftop viewpoint. The only buildings are simple round shelters used for cooking, and a couple of even simpler toilets – essentially concrete structures with holes in the ground. Our tent is already set up, with a folding table and chairs nearby. Our cook, Estefen, and his assistant Melaku welcome us with tea and popcorn. We could get used to this. It's a far cry from our usual hiking trips where, after walking all day, we still have to set up camp then think about cooking.

Thick-billed ravens are never far away, especially in the campsites where they are always on the lookout for unattended food. Found only in Ethiopia, the aptly named black bird has a substantial bill that looks as if it could bite through steel. We're careful not to go even a short distance away when there's food on our table. But at Sankaber we forget about a brand new bar of soap near the wash basin. Without warning, a raven soon swoops in, grabs it, and flies off.

Just as the sun sets, Estefen brings out our supper. He's dressed in his chef's hat and white jacket, an incongruous sight in this wilderness setting, but a nice touch. A candle stuck inside a cut-off plastic water bottle provides light and adds a splash of elegance to our first meal in the mountains.

We're suitably attired for dining, meaning that we're wearing every piece of clothing we have with us. It may be hot shirt-sleeve weather as we hike during the day, but as soon as the sun goes down, the temperature drops like a rock at this altitude. We quickly don sweaters, warm coats, hats, and gloves. At night we sleep in wool long johns inside our down sleeping bags. When we wake next morning, our thermometer shows about 0 degrees Celsius. Not bad. Abiyot told us not to be surprised if we hit minus 5 degrees.

It is mostly guests who sleep in tents. Some guides or other helpers have tents, but most simply make do. The cooks usually sleep in the cooking shelter. Most scouts and mule handlers stay outside, wrapped head to toe in the ubiquitous blankets that often take the place of coats.

Next morning the rest of our team arrives – two mules with two mule handlers. They will carry all the food, bottled drinking water, and camping and cooking gear between the three campsites we'll be visiting. We also hire a riding mule, which comes with a mule handler. This was an option we debated, but decided that one mule might be a good idea, just in case. We have concerns as to how well we'll hold up at high altitudes. A mule would come in handy if we suffered from altitude sickness, or one of us twisted an ankle or had some other mishap. Forget about calling an ambulance for pickup where we're headed.

The terrain gets progressively rougher past Sankaber. A narrow ridge takes us to a lookout point, next to the appropriately named Geech Abyss, where the land drops into nothingness. Across the narrow gorge we look over a waterfall, now a mere trickle in the bone dry conditions, with a single drop of a half kilometre straight down.

We watch lammergeyers soaring effortlessly in the thermals, some flying far below us in the deep chasms. These magnificent birds stay with us throughout the trip. Also known as bearded vultures, they have wingspans close to three metres. While this rare species lives in mountain areas in various parts of Africa, Asia, and Europe, their biggest populations are in Ethiopia. Like most vultures, lammergeyers are scavengers, living mostly on dead creatures. But they have very discriminating tastes, with a preference for bone marrow. Their digestive systems can handle smaller bones, but for big bones they have a special trick. They pick up a bone, fly a hundred metres or more into the air, then drop it on rocks, making it easier to get at the nutritious marrow in the shattered pieces.

We're enjoying the view until Getachew tells us that we have to cross that gorge. The good news is that we can walk downhill for a while. The bad news is that we have to climb back up even higher. As it turns out, walking downhill on the rocky trail proves to be every bit as difficult. There's less huffing and puffing than going up, but more strain on our knees. We rely on our walking sticks to keep from slipping down the loose dusty soil. No chance of riding the mule; it too has its challenges in the uneven rugged sections.

The terrain levels out at the bottom as we follow a river valley, then stop for lunch at an idyllic spot with rocky outcroppings above a little waterfall. Tired from the walk, we stretch out on the pancake rocks for a short snooze. Then it's time for our regular ritual of slathering on more sunscreen almost every time we stop. At higher altitudes, UV radiation becomes a lot more intense, so we face an ongoing battle to prevent sunburn.

It's hard to leave this beautiful spot, especially when we look at the trail and know that it's all uphill from here. While we're resting and enjoying the view, we watch the mule train go by. We left Sankaber early in the morning, right after breakfast. In the meantime, the cooks and mule handlers had packed up camp, and are now passing us. The mules are carrying all the gear: tents, bedrolls, chairs, tables, propane tanks, cooking utensils, and boxes of food. Not only our mules, but those from other camping groups pass by in a line, stopping every now and then while handlers adjust loads that are constantly shifting on the rough uneven trail.

Despite this being a national park, villages dot the landscape, with even more communities around the park periphery. Throughout our trek, we see people herding sheep, goats, and cattle. Cultivated crop land covers slopes that would make a mountain goat dizzy. Increased erosion, overgrazing, and other human pressures are taking a toll on native plants and animals – the very reasons this place was designated a national park and World Heritage Site in the first place. The impact is serious enough that UNESCO has put the Simien Mountains on its List of World Heritage Sites in Danger. Our path takes us beside a man breaking new land, a formidable task using an ox pulling a primitive wooden plow through ground that seems more rock than soil. It's a shame to see even more native grassland destroyed, but his family has to eat.

There's no easy solution. People have lived here for over 2,000 years, long before the national park was declared. The government is encouraging mountain dwellers to move by offering to buy them out. From stories we hear, a major gap remains between what is being offered and what they would accept as a settlement. This won't happen quickly, if at all. Even if the villagers agreed to move, where would they go in this already overcrowded country?

Our approach to Geech village looks surreal. The settlement

sprawls across the hillside – an assortment of round buildings of rocks and mud, topped with substantial thatched roofs. In most rural villages in Africa, we usually see corrugated tin or other trappings, however simple, from the modern world. Looking at Geech from across the valley, there is absolutely nothing to remind us that we are still in the present, that we haven't somehow been transported a thousand years back in time. The community survives on farming, but we see no farming equipment. Men are winnowing grain by hand, tossing seeds in the air, allowing chaff to be carried away by the afternoon breeze.

The campground just past Geech sits on an exposed windswept plateau. We arrive completely exhausted. After an hour or so of rest (accompanied, of course, by the customary hot tea and popcorn), Getachew tells us that this is by far the best place to see sunset. There's just one glitch – the viewpoint is a bit of a walk away, uphill of course. We trudge up the long slope to the edge of a precipice dropping into dark shadows. While the setting would be spectacular anytime, the lingering evening light casts a magical glow across the slopes and peaks. Haze covers the horizon, diffusing streaks of warm light over the wild land.

Next morning, we're ready to leave, but there's a minor problem – the riding mule has disappeared. Sometime in the night or early morning, it decided it had had enough, and turned for home. We start out anyway, while the mule handler, Kelebie, looks for the runaway. After an hour or so, they catch up to us, poor Kelebie apologizing profusely for his mule's bad behaviour.

We come across our first band of geladas, commonly called gelada baboons. Scientists tell us that these primates are closely related to baboons, but are separate animals. Found only in the highlands of Ethiopia, geladas are the world's highest dwelling primates, and the most terrestrial of all primates, other than humans. Unlike most other baboons and monkeys, they only rarely venture into trees. Geladas are grass-eaters, preferring to walk and shuffle along the ground where they pick blades of grass with their hands. They also live in larger groups than other baboons, with some bands topping 300 animals.

Our immediate impression is how gentle and easy-going they seem. In other parts of Africa, we would never even consider approaching a group of baboons. Here, if we stand in one spot in the general direction they are heading, they will walk right beside us and barely give us more than a bemused look. At first glance, the big males appear imposing and fairly intimidating. They have hair to spare – luxuriant, golden, and shaggy lion-like manes. The males' cape of hair covers them so completely, that when they sit still in the grass, they almost look like small haystacks. Occasionally males open their mouths wide and roll back their lips to display sharp teeth – a threatening gesture often used by competing males.

Geladas are called the "Bleeding Heart Baboon" for the red, heart-shaped hairless patch on their chests. Females ready to mate display a brighter red patch, an obvious signal to waiting males. They often "talk" to each other, with fairly high-pitched tones a favourite of their varied repertoire of calls. Some sounds made by baby geladas are remarkably like cries of human babies.

The geladas move on, and reluctantly, so do we. It's time to continue our upward climb along the mountain slope to a 4,000-metre ridge. Now, we're especially glad that we arranged for our mule. The route turns out to be a steady heart-thumping, lung-gasping grunt, every step uphill in the oxygen starved air. We take turns riding the mule for 20 minutes or so then change off. Getachew and Jemale climb steadily as if this is just another stroll in the park.

At the summit we stop for a rest and can see forever in every direction. Chenek campground looms in the distance, far below. This is the steepest descent of all, along a series of eroded switchbacks and goat trails. In the valley we see a few thatched-roofed buildings in a village, cultivated land reaching way up the opposite slope, and the road where a truck looks like a toy. Several times, the trail skirts the edge of the escarpment, with views that continually bring the camera out of the bag.

Chenek is not only a campground, but also a tiny village where men working for the national park live with their families. Jemale points out his house, and not long after we arrive, his two young kids come running over to greet him. Since he lives just up the hill across the road, we assume that he'll be sleeping there during our two-night stay at Chenek. But no, he insists that he guard our tent. It's his job, so he'll stay. He sleeps on a broken concrete bench outside, his trusty Kalashnikov beside him.

Since we have an extra day at Chenek, we plan on hiking toward Mount Bwahit, its summit reaching over 4,400 metres. Every day as we set out on our hike, we can't imagine that the impressive scenery could get any better, but it does. Today we stop to take in the incredible view in one direction over the yawning chasms below, and twenty minutes later, we discover another unforgettable view facing a different direction. It continues like this for the next hour as we climb steadily along the edge of the escarpment. Stopping for another well-deserved rest, we overlook a cliff face with an opening to a cave on one side.

"I'd like to see what's in that cave," says Getachew.

"You'd be nuts to go there!" we tell him. We see no clear route to the opening that drops into a deep nasty canyon.

But there's no stopping him. Getachew is always very careful when guiding us, and never puts us in dangerous situations, but when he's by himself, he becomes a daredevil, totally unafraid of heights, and oblivious to dangerous precipices. We watch him nimbly climb like a mountain goat over places that make us wince.

This time, even easy-going Jemale, never fazed by anything, yells a warning in Amharic, but to no avail. Getachew makes it safely to the cave and back, with the help of some fancy rock-climbing acrobatics.

"He belongs in the crazy hospital in Addis!" says Jemale, shaking his head in resignation.

As we climb to over 4,200 metres, we're really feeling the lack of oxygen, and have to rest more often. We're on the lookout for rare Walia ibex, and the area around Chenek is considered the best bet to find them. Getachew tells us they usually frequent sheltered valleys rather than open areas at higher altitudes, so we decide to spend the rest of the day looking for ibex rather than continuing higher.

Getachew suggests a particular valley where he occasionally sees them, and to get there we have to cross the road that winds through the high mountain pass. Ahead of us, a three-ton truck slowly crawls up the hill, the box on the back packed with people. This is public transport. A bus from Debark comes part way into the mountains, but higher up, a heavy duty truck takes over. Barely moving, it finally stops. Everyone climbs out and starts walking up the steep road. The truck doesn't have enough power to make the hill because there isn't enough oxygen for the motor to run properly. Now it's stalled. Each time the driver tries to start it, a deafening backfire echoes through the hills, followed by a great cloud of blue smoke. After several tries, the engine finally starts, and the truck continues its snail's-pace climb, eventually catching up to its passengers.

We scour the valleys and eventually spot a few ibex far below. Found nowhere else in the world but the Simien Mountains, Walia ibex are highly endangered, with only about 500 animals left. The large, regal-looking goat-like animals are an attractive chestnut brown and grey, with white on the legs and undersides. The defining feature of the males is their thick horns that curl back for a metre or more in graceful curves. The ibex we see are all females, with much smaller and thinner horns. They're too far away to photograph.

Approaching the campground in late afternoon, we're resigned to the fact that we likely won't get close to ibex, since we're leaving the next morning. Then someone runs over to find us. There's ibex nearby. We make our way to the bluffs where they were last spotted, then suddenly catch sight of two big magnificent males grazing calmly less than 50 metres away. They eventually move into a clearing and cooperate long enough for photos. Even more impressive close-up, they sport long goatee beards and lethal-looking horns used to battle each other for dominance.

We're doing quite well for finding rare critters, so we're not too disappointed when we fail to find the most elusive animal of all – the Ethiopian wolf. It's the world's rarest wild canid, or dog-like animal, and Africa's most endangered carnivore. Numbering just 300–400 animals in total, they are found only in isolated mountain areas of Ethiopia, with most in the Bale Mountains farther south. The Simien Mountains are thought to have about 50. We've come close, however. On our last morning at Chenek, a couple guides tell us that they heard wolves during the night.

Before we pack to leave, Jemale invites us to his house for coffee. Drinking coffee is one of the joys of travelling in Ethiopia. No matter where we go – fancy city restaurant, small town cafe,

Estefen's hearty breakfasts at our mountain-top campsites – the coffee is always great. Perhaps not surprising considering that Ethiopia is where the stuff originated.

While the exact origins of coffee are lost in time, legends abound. A common story is that of a goat herder in the highlands of Ethiopia who noticed that when his animals ate the berries from a particular tree, they became more spirited. Trying some himself, the herder was amazed at how alert he felt. He took some of the wondrous berries to the abbot at a local monastery, but the holy man disapproved and threw the berries into the fire. When they smelled the wonderful aroma that came from the burning berries, the abbot had a change of heart, and retrieved the berries from the fire. They dissolved the roasted berries in hot water, and the first cup of coffee was born. It's such a wonderful story that if it didn't happen exactly that way, it should have.

Coffee at Jemale's very modest house is no exception to the rule of taking coffee seriously. His wife goes through the whole traditional coffee ceremony, starting with raw beans that she washes a number of times in warm water. Then she roasts the beans in a shallow frying pan over a small charcoal fire – an important part of the ceremony is appreciating the aroma of the roasting beans. She pounds the beans using a mortar and pestle then puts the powder in the coffee pot with hot water to brew. It doesn't get any fresher than this. Jemale's neighbours wander in and out to share in the coffee and conversation. It's considered good manners to have at least three cups during a coffee ceremony, so at the end we're buzzed and ready for anything.

But today we have nothing more strenuous than the long and dusty bone-jarring drive to Debark, then back to Gonder. Catching our last glance of these mountains, we agree that this ranks among the high points of our travels. Breathtaking landscapes on the Roof of Africa, extraordinary wildlife, fascinating cultures, agreeable travel companions – all served up with the world's best coffee.

Sleeping with Rhinos
Close Encounters with Africa's Big Five

Rhino in the campground at Marakele National Park.

The two-ton monster stares at us through the front door of our tiny tent, its long curved horn pointing like a dagger. If that's not enough to stir us from slumber, four of its buddies have us surrounded. Without warning a scuffle breaks out, sending bits of gravel flying against our tent. Never again will we complain about not getting close enough to rhinos.

Rhinoceros are among Africa's fabled Big Five, along with elephants, African buffalo, lions, and leopards. The Big Five list originated with the old safari hunters of Africa. Of all the animals they hunted, these five could fight back, and were considered the most dangerous. Today's safari hunters are more likely armed with binoculars and cameras, but the allure of finding the Big Five remains. Potential dangers also remain.

In major wildlife areas, such as South Africa's Kruger National Park, you can generally find the Big Five, but seeing all of them is never guaranteed. Elephants and buffalo seem to be everywhere. Spend enough time in the park, and you will almost certainly see lions. Most difficult to find is the elusive and secretive leopard. Even South Africans who frequently visit the park say that they see leopards only on rare occasions.

Wildlife viewing is seldom predictable. Kruger National Park is roughly the size of Wales or Israel, with animals moving around freely. During our first trip to this famous park, the most elusive animal is, surprisingly, our first Big Five sighting. Less than an hour after entering the park, we see something ahead sitting on the side of the road. Grabbing the binoculars, we confirm that it is what we hope – a young leopard. We inch the car slowly forward, hoping not to spook the animal before we get within camera range. Just before we're close enough, the cat scampers across the road. It stops, turns around and looks at us for about two seconds, just long enough to fire off a couple shots. Then we catch a quick glimpse of something else moving in the bushes, and know why the small cat was headed that way. Its mother is hidden under some branches in a thorny thicket. Almost immediately, both of them melt into the dense bush.

That's our first and only leopard sighting during 13 days

in the park. We see mind-boggling numbers of wildlife – giraffes, zebras, hippos, hyenas, jackals, warthogs, monkeys, baboons, wildebeest, impalas, kudus...the list goes on. The phenomenal birdlife includes everything from enormous eagles, hawks, and herons to brilliant rollers and bee-eaters looking like they've been dipped in paint. Most of the Big Five reveal themselves – elephants and buffalo galore, and a fair number of lions. Rhinos, however, elude us. The odd ones we glimpse are either far in the distance, or completely obscured by dense vegetation. It isn't until our last day in the park that a lone male white rhino saunters out of the bush to graze close to the road.

The largest and most numerous of the world's five rhino species, everything about the "white" is massive, from its weight that can top two and a half tons, length up to four metres, and folded skin resembling armour plating. Despite the name, the white rhino isn't white, but a medium grey that is similar in colour to its smaller cousin, the black rhino, which likewise isn't black. It was Dutch settlers who named the bigger rhino for its wide mouth that is tailor-made for grazing. The black rhino, on the other hand, has a narrower pointed upper lip that's better suited to browsing leaves. Somewhere along the way, the English word white came into use, since it sounds similar to the Dutch word for wide.

The gargantuan grass-eating machine seems to completely ignore us as he munches steadily, his heavy head seldom leaving the ground. It's a long, curious-looking head, topped by ears that stick straight up, eyes that are unusually low set, and great curved horns that are both its defining feature and its curse. Watching and photographing this fascinating creature is a highlight of the trip, leaving us with a taste for more.

We get our wish. Future trips to Kruger as well as to other

parks reward us with exceptional rhino encounters. At Crocodile Bridge, the southern-most rest camp of Kruger Park, a half dozen or so rhinos, including a mother and half-grown calf, stay close by and show themselves every day, occasionally stopping traffic as they slowly wander across the road.

Hluhluwe-Imfolozi Park in South Africa's KwaZulu Natal province near the Indian Ocean has a special link with rhinos, both as an excellent place to find them today and for its historic role in bringing these animals back from the brink of extinction. Rhinos were once common to many parts of Africa, but during the 20th century, they came close to disappearing. Work done here in protecting the rhinos, then relocating animals to repopulate other parks, is credited with much of their resurgence in numbers. Today, Africa has around 20,000 rhinos, with over 90% in South Africa. While this is only a fraction of their historic numbers, wildlife managers were encouraged that at least the trend was heading in the right direction.

Unfortunately, in recent years rhino poaching has reached alarming levels. In 2007, 13 rhinos were poached in South Africa. The number soared to 448 in 2011, then to 668 in 2012. The horns can be worth $60,000 per kilogram, more than their weight in gold. It's been called the most expensive illegal substance in the world. Rhino horns have long been prized for dagger handles in parts of the Middle East, but the most serious threat comes from demand in Asia where rhino horn is thought to have medicinal properties. Increasing affluence in Southeast Asia, and especially in Vietnam, has spurred a thriving and lucrative black market. Despite the claims of medicinal properties, scientists say that consuming rhino horn, which is composed of keratin, has about the same medicinal value as eating fingernails. Newscasts are filled with reports of shoot-outs between park rangers and highly sophisticated bands of poachers. The situation has become so critical that it is thought that, after many years of success in restoring rhino numbers, they may once again be headed for the brink.

The poaching problem is never far behind the scenes in the parks. Armed rangers patrol, but in huge parks such as Kruger, they can't be everywhere at once. We stop at the Pufuri Picnic Site in the far northern reaches of Kruger Park and chat with the attendant living on site. This looks like an idyllic job, living on the bank overlooking the Luvuvhu River in the midst of some of the most gorgeous countryside, surrounded by wildlife. Idyllic on the surface, yes, but he confesses that his biggest worry is being shot by poachers if they ever decide to come this way.

Another change in recent years has been to the "sightings boards", a fixture in most wildlife parks in South Africa. These are bulletin board-sized maps of the park's road network. Each major wildlife species is assigned a coloured magnet (red for lions, yellow for leopards, and so on), so when guests return to camp, they can indicate where they saw various animals by putting a coloured magnet on the approximate area. This in turn helps other visitors learn where wildlife has been seen. The magnets for rhinos have been removed; it was just too easy for poachers to benefit from this information.

More than anywhere in Africa, wildlife parks in South Africa are well set up for independent, do-it-yourself wildlife viewing. Heavily used by South Africans, the parks have developed infrastructure making it fairly easy to drive on your own, and stay in park rest camps which often have a variety of accommodation ranging from swanky air-conditioned bungalows to simple huts to campgrounds. While many visitors tour around on guided safari excursions, we much prefer the freedom of the do-it-yourself option, deciding where we want to go and spending as much time as we like in a spot. All visitors have to be back in camp during strictly enforced gate closing times, which more or less coincide with sunrise and sunset. To see any of the park after dark, the only option is taking a guided excursion operated by the park.

In wildlife parks, you are allowed to get out of your car only at designated spots. The reasons are obvious – you could be eaten. But even in the relative safety of your car, you have to be careful around certain animals. While lions are the predators that immediately spring to mind, lions and other big cats tend not to be a threat if you stay in your car. Lions have often walked right beside our car, where they would be close enough to reach out and touch (not a good idea). While most other animals don't like to get too close to people, lions aren't afraid of anything, including people and their cars. They go where they want, when they want. If they happen to think that now is a good time to take a nap in the middle of the road, that's exactly what they'll do. Let the traffic go around.

Buffalo, weighing up to two tons, have to be given a wide berth, especially old males on their own that tend to be grumpy and bad-tempered. You don't want to be on the receiving end of their thick horns that resemble battering rams adorned with sharp points.

The animals we worry about most when driving are elephants. They appear docile and easy-going as they move, usually slowly, while browsing the bushes. But you never know what they might do. There's a widely circulating video on YouTube showing an elephant-car confrontation at Pilanesberg Game Reserve. Elephants are walking down the road toward the car, and the driver stops and waits for the elephants to pass by (another not so good idea). Without warning, one of the elephants takes a dislike to the car, and effortlessly pushes it to the side and rolls it over.

Occasionally elephants show obvious signs of aggression. We see a prime example at a waterhole in Addo Elephant National Park. Workers are at the waterhole with a backhoe doing some digging and maintenance. When a group of females and young arrive, they sense something out of the ordinary and quickly move on. Then a lone male comes by, one of the biggest elephants we've ever seen. Obviously shocked and appalled at the disturbance, he shakes his head violently, flaps his ears, flings his trunk, and moves as if he doesn't know where to lash out. We move out of this guy's way in a hurry.

If elephants are feeding right beside the road, we often have to wait until they move back before we attempt to drive by. One time in Kruger National Park we come around a corner on a minor road to find a herd of elephants crossing almost immediately in front of us. No problem, we'll just back up to give them some room and wait it out. But as we start backing up, there's the other half of the herd crossing right behind us. We're sandwiched in the middle with nowhere to go. They take their time crossing, and fortunately ignore us.

Rhinos don't tend to be aggressive to people or cars, but here too, you never know. They usually move slowly, but can run close to 60 km/hour. A few years ago a friend returned from South Africa with a story of a black rhino that attacked a car. It rammed its long sharp horn into the front of the car, got it jammed in the radiator, and couldn't get it free. In frustration it shook its head up and down, lifting the car part way up each time, until it finally shook itself loose. Black rhinos have a reputation for being more unpredictable and bad-tempered, while the larger and more numerous white rhinos are generally more temperate.

We have never felt threatened by a rhino when driving through wildlife parks, although we're also careful to keep a respectful distance. On a trip to Pilanesberg Game Reserve, we see rhinos every day, but each time they are either too far away or hidden behind thick vegetation for good photos. Sometimes you have to be careful what you wish for. One day we're driving along a twisting minor road through dense bush, doing no more than 20 km/hour. Coming around a sharp turn, we suddenly drive right into a small group of rhinos. We're not sure who is more startled, us or them. At the same instant, they quickly jump off both sides of the road and we back up in a hurry. Fortunately, they don't turn aggressive and soon continue grazing, while we wait far back until they wander away from the road.

It's more than the Big Five that visitors are after. Cheetahs are another favourite, the fastest animals in the world, capable of short bursts of speed over 100 km/hour. While they primarily hunt early or late in the day, they also hunt more often in the daytime than other big cats. This doesn't mean that they're easy to find. While not as elusive as leopards, sightings are always special.

Among the most sought-after wildlife, outside of the Big Five, is the African wild dog. Once widespread throughout sub-Saharan Africa, they are now among the most endangered animals, with an estimated total population of little more than 5,000 in the entire continent. About the size of a border collie, they are a beautiful mottled black, white, yellow, and brown. Sometimes called "painted wolves", they are completely different creatures from both wolves or domestic dogs.

Considered the most social of all canids or dog-like animals, wild dogs are almost always in groups. They hunt cooperatively as a pack. We are fortunate to come across them occasionally in Kruger National Park, usually resting and sleeping right beside the road. One evening we find a pack only a half-hour before the gates close for the evening. We don't have much time, but we have them all to ourselves, with no other cars around. They're playing on and near the road, wrestling with each other, grooming, and just wandering around. They are so close that we could reach out to touch them (definitely not a good idea). You could be fooled into thinking that they're just cute puppy dogs. But when they open their mouths to yawn, the powerful jaws reveal rows of brilliant white sharp teeth, tailor-made for tearing things to bits.

Dogs usually hunt in early morning or evening, but in Hluhluwe-Imfolozi Park we happen across a pack of 22 on the hunt during a cool rainy afternoon. Coming to a crossroad, we see the pack run past on the other road. We follow as they run slowly for a while, stop for a few seconds while some dogs make brief forays into the bush, then quickly return to the road. They are being very quiet; it's obvious that they are after something. This goes on for two or three kilometres, then just ahead of the dogs, a couple impala are spooked and try making a run for it. The chase is on, as the dogs spread out to attack from different angles. The first impala practically takes flight as it makes a powerful leap across the road with unbelievable speed and barely escapes. The second one isn't so lucky. The dogs hit it in mid-leap and several converge on it, seemingly tearing it to pieces before it even hits the ground. No longer quiet, the dogs growl as if in a feeding frenzy; individuals quickly make off with various parts. One dog disappears carrying a leg, while two others rip apart innards, their faces dripping red with blood.

The only other vehicle around is a truck driven by a researcher who is studying wild dogs. Talking to her afterwards brings home just how unusual our encounter has been. After tracking this pack for several months, this is the first time she's seen them make a kill close to the road. A rare encounter with life and death in the African bush.

In most South African wildlife parks, the rest camps are fenced with electric wires so you can sleep with the assurance that nothing will eat you or trample you in the middle of the night. Some rest camps, such as in Hluhluwe-Imfolozi Park and parts of Kgalagadi Transfrontier Park in the Kalahari Desert, have unfenced rest camps. But these consist of fixed-roof accommodation such as chalets, or fairly substantial safari tents with slightly raised wooden platforms, and attached kitchens and bathrooms so you don't have to go out at night.

So it is with our safari tent at Impila Camp in Hluhluwe-Imfolozi Park. Because it's unfenced, various critters occasionally wander by – zebra, nyala, and especially impala. One day we see a group of a dozen or so impala relaxing in the shade, only 10 metres away.

The barbecue stand is on the ground, just down from the platform deck between the main part of the tent and the kitchen. Our first evening there, we put skewers of meat on the barbecue, and keep a close eye while sitting on the deck, no more than two metres away. It didn't take long; just a couple moments of inattention while refilling a wine glass. Turning back to the barbecue, we look in horror as a fully grown spotted hyena, its gaping powerful mouth wide open, is about to clamp down on our supper. We both start yelling and it immediately takes off, its nose bumping the grill a bit, definitely upset at being forced to leave without its almost stolen meal. The following nights, we stay close to the barbecue, never taking our eyes off it. The hyena makes the rounds every night, quietly lurking in the shadows and watching to assess its chances before moving on to the next camp. It probably makes an easy living, since sizzling meat on the "braai" is practically mandatory for South Africans on holiday. The park posts warning signs to watch out for hyenas, and not to feed them, but there's bound to be somebody not paying close attention.

As a general rule, campgrounds where you can pitch your own tent are only located in fenced rest camps in South African wildlife parks. Marakele National Park, in the Waterberg Mountains north of Pretoria, is an exception. A fence divides the two areas of the park. One part has all of the Big Five – a mountainous, heavily forested area where the only accommodation is permanent safari tents.

A wildlife highlight in this section is seeing the world's largest colony of endangered cape vultures. To get there we follow a long, winding, and steep one-lane road to the top of the highest mountain. The road is so narrow that it takes some tricky manoeuvring to pass an oncoming car without going over the edge. Fortunately, traffic is light. Not only do we have sweeping views from the top, but also have a reasonably close look at these increasingly rare birds. Cape vultures are among Africa's bigger raptors, found only in the southern part of the continent. With wingspans that can stretch over eight feet, they effortlessly soar high above the mountain tops, occasionally swooping down if they spot something edible.

The other part of the park is in the Kwaggasvlakte Plains, with a wide variety of wildlife, but just one of the Big Five – rhinos. The only accommodation option here is an unfenced campground. We set up our tent among the other tents, trailers, and truck campers, and can't help but notice that ours is the smallest tent by far. The campground looks over a waterhole in the distance, and throughout the afternoon we watch animals come and go, mostly zebra and kudus. Since there are no big predators such as lions and leopards, the wildlife tends to be more relaxed and less afraid. Slowly but surely, some animals make their way into the campground. Ostrich are the most common visitors. Quite bold, they wander fairly close to people, always on the lookout for unattended food. These flightless birds seem even bigger and more imposing close up, their heads stretching nine feet or nearly three metres above the ground.

Close to evening, we see a mother rhino and half-grown calf drinking at the waterhole. We set up our longest telephoto lens and start photographing as they slowly munch on grass practically non-stop. They keep walking in our direction, and soon we have to switch to a shorter lens. Eventually, they walk right to the edge of the campground. Most campers gather around to watch, and the rhinos look back, making it difficult to know who is watching whom. Finally, the rhinos get bored and slowly disappear into the forest.

We're thrilled with this close encounter. But when we chat with the campers next to us, we learn that this was pretty tame. Bryan and Liz are from Cape Town, and have already been here for a couple days. They tell us that the night before, rhinos walked right into camp and grazed next to their tent. For some reason, the rhinos have decided that the campground is an integral part of their daily grazing route, even though there's plenty of grass elsewhere.

Going to sleep, we assume that the rhinos have had their campground visit that day and are off exploring greener pastures. It's still dark at 4:00 am, but we awake to obvious crunching noises and footsteps of something big. Really big. The rhinos are back, grazing just outside, the sound very much like cattle eating grass, only louder. The weather is hot, so we've left all the tent flaps open, with only thin mosquito screen between us and the outside world.

We count five monsters surrounding our tent. Rhinos look imposing anytime, but a sight we'll never forget is looking up at them while we're lying on the ground.

The huge animals aren't at all aggressive, and fortunately they are walking around the tents rather than over them. Then suddenly a scuffle breaks out right in front of our tent. Why, we don't know. There's snorting and stamping of feet so close that bits of gravel splatter on the front of the tent. Looking out, we see one rhino facing us, its lethal horn pointed directly at us. The next campsite has a light on, so when the rhino turns sideways, the profile of the curved horn throws a shadow that completely fills our tent door. It feels like something straight out of an Alfred Hitchcock movie, like the knife about to slash through the shower curtain. There is nothing we can do but wait it out and hope for the best. Fortunately, the animals soon quiet down, continue munching grass for a few more minutes, then eventually wander off. It takes longer for our heart rates to quiet down.

So what would sane, rational people do when faced with such an experience? We're not sure what they would do. We, on the other hand, decide to stay another night. But tonight, it's time to reinforce the campsite. We park the car immediately next to the tent. On the opposite side, we roll the remains of a dead tree trunk with a protruding branch. At the back of the tent, we put up our lawn chairs, then break out laughing as we think about the absurdity of it all. Yeah, right, nothing like flimsy lawn chairs to stop raging rhinos dead in their tracks! But all we're trying to do is discourage them from standing too close to the tent while grazing, and judging from last night's visit, they weren't disturbing anything around camp. As we look around the sites, other campers have devised similar "barriers".

We sleep most of the night, then suddenly awake to a commotion outside. It's the distinctive call of zebras, their strange yelp sounding somewhat like a dog with hiccups. Several of the striped horse-like creatures walk through the campground, and are having an argument among themselves.

The sun is shining next time we awake. Looking out the front of the tent, we see that the rhinos are back, six of them this time, grazing on the edge of the campground but slowly working their way toward us. As they inch closer, we decide it's safest to get out of the tent and be ready to jump into the car if they come too close. Slowly but surely they keep coming – munch, munch, closer, closer. One male rhino about 10 metres away looks up and stares straight at us. We get in the car, as he continues to stare. Clearly, something about us is either troubling him or making him curious. After an uncomfortably long time of staring, he resumes eating and they all slowly move on.

Later we have tea with Liz and Bryan in the next site who had slept through that morning's visitation while the rhinos grazed beside their tent. We mention that we'll be moving on that afternoon.

"Oh, we were hoping you'd stay longer," says Liz. "Now we'll have the smallest tent!"

CATS OF THE KALAHARI
Languid Lions and Leaping Leopards

Lion on a Kalahari sandbank.

The Kalahari Desert sprawls over a million square kilometres of southern Africa, much of it in Botswana where it covers most of the country, along with extensive parts of northern South Africa and eastern Namibia. Smaller chunks encroach into Angola, Zambia, and Zimbabwe. It holds the largest expanse of sand in the world, stabilized in semi-arid, sandy savanna, alternating with open red dunes that fade into infinity. There is some debate as to whether or not the Kalahari should even be called a desert, since parts have more rainfall than do true deserts. But there's no question that it's damn dry, and where we're going in the southern Kalahari, is among the driest parts.

Kgalagadi Transfrontier Park straddles the border of South Africa and Botswana, an International Peace Park combining former national parks of both countries. Known as the Great Thirstland, it's a stark though beautiful expanse of red sand and thickets, with more greenery along the river valleys. Well...sort of rivers. The Auob and Nossob River Valleys run through the park, the latter marking the border between the two countries. These ephemeral waterways are rivers in theory, but only contain water every 25–100 years. Yet there's enough moisture for grasses and a variety of other plants and shrubs. While trees are not plentiful, the valleys boast magnificent stands of camelthorn trees, some growing over 15 metres tall. The trees are favourite haunts of leopards that sometimes rest in the shade on branches high in the canopy, or stash their prey out of reach of scavengers. The leaves are a favoured food for giraffes, which somehow get their tongues around the barbwire thorns.

We stop at Auchterlonie waterhole along the Auob River Valley where an attractive old stone house with a thatched roof has been restored and turned into a museum. It tells the story of waterholes that dot the valley, many of which go back to World War I, and were developed not for wildlife, but for the military. At the time, neighbouring Namibia was a German colony. South African and British troops had planned to invade Namibia and had mapped a route across the Kalahari Desert, since the Germans would not be expecting them to come this way. In preparation, they drilled a series of wells to provide a water supply for the troops. Guards were stationed at each well to keep them operating.

In the end, this invasion route was abandoned, and the guards at the wells were given the chance to stay and establish farms, which some did. Reality soon set in for those who stayed. Raising livestock in the desert was a daunting task. The homesteaders eventually gave up, then in 1931 the area became part of South Africa's Kalahari Gemsbok National Park. In 1999, the national parks on both the South Africa and Botswana sides combined to become Kgalagadi Transfrontier Park, one of Africa's larger parks. The waterholes are still there, now used extensively by wildlife.

We're immediately struck by how much wildlife thrives in this dry thirsty land. Most obvious are the large herds of springbok – slender, beautiful tan and white antelope only found in the arid westerly parts of southern Africa. Specially adapted to the dry conditions, they can go without drinking water if it is not available, surviving on moisture in the plants they eat. The most abundant antelope of the region, the springbok is the national animal of South Africa, and the name of that country's famous national rugby team. Springbok have the ability to jump or "pronk" when running – a strange stiff-legged bounce, as if their legs are spring-loaded, carrying them as much as four metres in a single bound. Pronking is a tactic often used to elude predators, but we watch as several young calves pronk for no apparent reason, probably just for fun, and just because they can.

Springbok herds are the fast food outlets for the big cats of the Kalahari. While lions and leopards prefer bigger and meatier prey such as wildebeest or gemsbok, springbok are plentiful and nearly always available, perfect for the times you feel like a nice light snack. Springbok is the food of choice for cheetahs, which have a difficult time bringing down heavier animals, but have the necessary speed to catch these fast agile antelope.

Not surprising, springbok are always alert and looking around. Every time we come across a grazing herd, we spot sentries posted at the outer edges. Their job is to keep a constant eye out in case predators try to sneak up. We pass a camelthorn tree where a dozen or so young calves lie together in the shade, a springbok day-care centre, where the little ones are gathered together and guarded for added protection. While springbok breed throughout the year, they time most births for around February or March, since this is usually when rains come and food is most abundant.

We happen upon a springbok giving birth right beside the road. When the mother drops the calf, she immediately starts cleaning it up and within a few minutes helps it to stand. It's quite a chore for the little guy as he wobbles from side to side and keeps falling back down. Once up, the mother quickly encourages the calf to walk and start moving. Springbok don't have the luxury of a prolonged childhood. They may have to start running at any moment, literally for their lives.

For the most part, the springbok herds look like one big happy family, although feuds do break out. Two males often get into tussles, but most times they're just testing their strength and aren't seriously hurt. But when a dominant male is challenged, things become intense. Around the corner from the main herd, we find two males battling it out, ramming and pushing so hard that they are both practically folded in half, their heads driven into the ground. They appear evenly matched, but eventually one prevails, chasing away his injured rival, blood dripping from his nose.

When blue wildebeest have a dust-up, the dust literally fills the air as hooves, fur, and horns fly fast and furious. The most serious wildebeest fight we see is right beside the waterhole at Nossob rest camp, where we watch and photograph from the comfort of a raised and protected blind overlooking the water. Wildebeest are well-suited to this dry country, needing water just every two or three days. But unlike some Kalahari animals, which can survive without water, wildebeest do have to drink eventually, and during severe droughts, they suffer most. Wildebeest visits to waterholes are usually uneventful, but this time a bull, an outsider, decides to wander in. The ensuing battle is both ferocious and prolonged, since the two bulls appear evenly matched. At times we can only barely make out the clash of horns in the flying dust, until finally the intruding bull is driven away.

This is the trip for battles; before long we see two male red hartebeest having a serious disagreement. These stately red-coloured antelope look completely at home as they blend into the red dunes. They're beautiful, sleek, but somewhat odd-looking, with long narrow faces that appear as if they've been squeezed in a vise. Both male and female have twisted horns rising straight above their heads, as if these too have been squeezed in a vise. First the two males chase each other at top speed, then ram head-on with such force that they both collapse on their front knees. One time when they lock horns, they are not only figuratively, but physically locked; they twist and turn wildly, trying to untangle their cork-screw-like horns.

The gemsbok is the most famous antelope of the Kalahari. Also known as an oryx, this striking animal is grey to tan in colour, accentuated with black patches and stripes, a long sweeping black tail, white "socks", and straight super sharp horns stretching up to a metre long. The overly long horns provide protection against predators, and males also use them when defending territory from competitors. As a bonus, they really come in handy when you need to scratch your rear end. These are true desert dwellers, able to survive without drinking water, and capable of adjusting their body temperature so as not to sweat in extreme heat. While they are a favourite food for lions, there have been cases of gemsbok stabbing lions with their rapier-like horns.

But the wildlife highlight, and main reason we're here, is the Kalahari's big cats – cheetahs, leopards, and lions. The black-maned male lions of the Kalahari are considered among the largest in Africa. They certainly look imposing, standing out in the open desert terrain. Compared to lions in Africa's bush land, these are more athletic because they cover long distances searching for prey, and their black manes look especially impressive because they don't get tattered in thick vegetation.

The Auob River Valley is among the top places in Africa to find cheetahs. Early one morning we approach a waterhole to see movement in the shrubs right beside the road. It's a cheetah struggling to pull a springbok it had just killed into the shade of a tree. It's difficult for cheetahs to drag their prey very far. Leopards will often haul their kills into tree branches where nothing else can reach it, and dine at their leisure. Cheetahs don't have this luxury, and this one is no exception. It immediately begins gulping down all it can as fast as possible, right on the spot, before scavengers inevitably show up. Barely stopping to catch her breath, the cat occasionally quickly glances around, its face dripping with blood. Jackals are soon on the scene, circling and waiting to close in. We're sitting in our car no more than five or six metres away, the cheetah paying us no heed. Eventually it is satiated and leaves, although the carcass is far from clean. Jackals move in, snatching bits of food and dashing away in case the cheetah comes back. What jackals don't grab, vultures will soon clean up.

Travelling from camp to camp, we keep running into Ben and Anita, a couple from South Africa's Limpopo province, who are travelling much the same route as we are. One morning as we're leaving for the day, they invite us to come to their campsite for a drink around 7:00 that evening. We wander over, find their campsite, but there's no one around, not even their car. This is very strange. It's past gate closing time when everyone has to be back in the rest camp. If you're out past closing time, and don't have a compelling reason, you can be fined.

It wasn't until the next day that we hear their story. They came upon a kill site right beside the road where cheetahs had downed a springbok. They stopped to watch the feasting and take photos, but when they were ready to move on, their car wouldn't start; it was completely dead. Getting out to check under the hood didn't seem like a good idea, since the cheetahs were too close. Eventually, another car came by, so Anita got a ride back to the rest camp to find help. Ben stayed with the car; the windows were down, and because they were power windows, there was no way to close them. Leaving a car here with open windows would be a tempting invitation for critters to investigate.

It was an easy fix when two men from the park arrived. The rough jarring roads had caused one of the battery cables to come off. Being close to cheetahs didn't cause any concern to the two guys who simply got out of the truck, waved their arms in the air, and yelled "shoo, shoo" at the cheetahs, which quickly ran off. They explained that cheetahs are usually fairly timid.

"But *never, ever* try that with leopards or lions," they warned.

Next morning we leave Twee Rivieren rest camp at dawn, on our way to the waterhole where we had seen the cheetah kill the previous morning. We pass several enormous camelthorn trees right beside the road, and suddenly catch a glimpse of movement high in the branches. We stop to watch, and soon an adult leopard emerges from the thick foliage and stretches out along a protruding branch, practically posing for us. It looks around, appears bored, then leaps effortlessly higher into the canopy. Our view is obscured by the vegetation, and by a sociable weaver nest that sprawls across the branches, looking like a haystack stuck in the tree. The leopard is so well hidden that all we can see is the tip of its tail hanging down. We wait for a while, but the tail never moves; it looks like the leopard has found a comfy spot where it will probably stay during the heat of the day. After exploring further, we stop in late afternoon to check out the tree again on our way back to the rest camp. Little has changed. As before, all we see is the tip of the tail, and only because we know where to look. For much of that day, people would have driven by, completely unaware that a leopard was lurking almost directly above them.

Wildlife is typically most active in early morning, then again in evening, especially during summer when temperatures often climb above 40 degrees Celsius. So whenever we see a big cat lying in the shade, chances are that it will be there for a while. One day about mid-morning we come across the biggest black-maned lion we have ever seen, sound asleep under a shady tree. We're anxious to photograph him, but it's pretty clear that he isn't going anywhere soon. So we decide to leave the slumbering cat, continue on to see what else we can find, then return in late afternoon. Eight hours later, the lion is still lying beside the same bush. It had only moved a few metres, as the sun and shade moved throughout the day.

The gates to our camp close in less than an hour, around sunset, and we still have to drive along a slow, extremely rough road. So we're hoping that the lion wakes up soon and perhaps goes for a drink at the nearby waterhole where we have staked out a good view. Eventually he begins to stir, rolls over, scratches his nose and yawns. He is obviously in no hurry to get up, and is completely oblivious to our timetable. Suddenly his big head pops up, his face showing that dazed look of someone who just woke up but hasn't yet had a jolt of coffee. He half sits up, yawns several more times, then shakes his enormous head and bushy mane. Finally, he starts walking. But instead of heading to the waterhole as we are hoping, he heads straight for the road, then decides to lie down right in the middle. We watch for a while, but clearly, he isn't budging. If we don't leave soon, we won't make it back before gate closing. Though the road is very narrow, we have no option but to drive around the lion, taking care not to run over his tail. He doesn't look up or even flinch as we go by.

Lions go where they please. We come across another waterhole where four lions are drinking. We not only have a prime vantage point for photography, but also the luxury of parking under a camelthorn tree, the only shade anywhere nearby. After drinking and grooming by the waterhole, the lions come walking straight toward us. At first we wonder what's happening. Are they curious? Do they want to chase us away? Soon it becomes clear that they could care less about us. It's the shade they want. The fact that we, along with four other cars are parked under the same tree doesn't faze them, and they settle down for a snooze. Another time at the same waterhole, a lioness brings her two young cubs to the shady spot, despite a half dozen cars being there as well. The cubs play but stay close to their mother, who doesn't seem to pay any attention to the cars and clicking cameras.

When cloudy weather moderates the heat somewhat, the wildlife becomes more active. Three large but not fully-grown male lions lounge beneath a tree. One gets up and decides to climb the tree, which has a straight trunk for the first couple metres or so, then a long sturdy branch running at about a 45-degree angle. Unlike leopards, lions are not natural tree climbers. He manages to make his way along the sloping branch, but looks awkward, his feet slipping to the side as he struggles for better grip. Then the fun starts – he can't figure out how to turn around, his lanky legs and big paws getting in the way. Eventually he works it out, carefully stepping over, and often tripping over, smaller branches and twigs on the way down. Then the other two lions each take a turn, with much the same results. The climbing doesn't have any obvious practical purpose – just three young guys hanging out and showing off to each other.

On the same cloudy day, we also notice a lone lioness walking slowly along the valley floor. A male soon appears, following a short distance behind. A male and female lion together often means that there's a good chance they could be mating. Sure enough, they settle down in the grass, rest for a while, then decide it's time. Copulation takes place fairly quickly, lasting less than a minute, but accompanied by growling and biting. The lioness rolls over with all fours in the air like a playful kitten, then they both sprawl out in the sand and have a nap. Fifteen minutes later, they're at it again. But this time when it's over, the lioness flattens her ears, bares her teeth and swats at her partner when he moves away.

Mating sessions can last several days, and during this time, the pair often stays in the same general area. We come back next morning and find that they haven't moved very far, only now they're behind some bushes that obscure our view. The bush likely has more to do with providing shade than a preference for privacy. Mating doesn't seem to affect lions' inclination to go where they want. Other times, we come across lions mating immediately beside the road, where they just ignore anyone watching them.

The park boasts one of the most diverse populations of raptors in Africa, including lappet-faced vultures, pygmy falcons, bataleurs, numerous pale chanting goshawks, and rarer martial eagles – the largest eagles in Africa. We seldom go a day without seeing ostriches, usually in pairs or small groups, but occasionally in herds of 40 or more. The world's biggest bird is well-suited to the dry landscape, getting by on moist plants when water isn't available. Several times we see a mother towering over her brood of recently hatched chicks. While they may look tiny in comparison to their mother, they are about the size of turkeys. Occasionally the mother spreads out a wing to provide shade so the babies don't overheat. We often come across kori bustards, the largest bird in the world capable of flight. Weighing up to 20 kilograms, these chunky birds prefer to walk through short grass and wooded savanna looking for insects, lizards, berries, and other tasty morsels. Because they're so heavy, it's tough for them to get airborne, so they usually fly only when necessary. We watch as one takes flight, putting a lot of effort into running and wing-flapping before taking off.

The oddest bird is the secretary bird, a raptor standing well over a metre tall with an eagle-like head and body, and long spindly legs covered in thick scales that are resistant to snake bites. That adaptation comes in handy, since these predatory birds search out snakes, lizards, and rodents, then stomp them to death with their powerful feet. Their name comes from the distinctive dark feathers that stick out from the backs of their heads, reminiscent of quill pens used by secretaries of old.

Usually we see secretary birds wandering alone across the plains, so it's not until they join other animals for a much needed drink at a waterhole that we realize how big they really are. They stand almost the same height as springbok, which are drinking alongside wildebeest. Wildebeest normally tolerate other wildlife, but they clearly don't like secretary birds, which they chase away anytime the birds come too close. In other wildlife parks, we always consider it a rare treat to find secretary birds, but there's so many in the Kalahari that we no longer stop to take photos unless they're doing something unusual. Talk about an embarrassment of riches.

Smaller critters abound, especially ubiquitous ground squirrels. Unlike most animals that seek out a shady spot in the heat of the day, ground squirrels continue to scurry around and forage for food. Their bushy tails are so huge that they often fold them over their heads, making perfect built-in umbrellas. Mongoose are common, especially the yellow mongoose that burrows in the sandy soil in rest camps and picnic sites. At Nossob, we spend a lot of time watching several of these little guys rushing around right outside our chalet.

We come across beautiful cape foxes on our drives, but the real find is the rarer bat-eared fox. The obvious name comes from their monstrous ears which look out of proportion to the rest of their bodies. Satellite-dish ears do come in handy in locating termites and other insects which make up their main diet. The bat-eared fox is depicted on the logo for Botswana National Parks.

Our favourite small animal, and most other visitors' favourite as well, is the meerkat. Found only in the western parts of southern Africa, this member of the mongoose family is a Kalahari specialist. Silvery brown and weighing less than a kilogram, these slender animals have a short snout that ends in a sharp tip. They are forever scurrying around digging for insects, worms, and anything else edible, but they are most famous for standing straight up to survey their surroundings. Whenever meerkats feed, they post one or more guards who stand up like they're on their tiptoes, usually on the ground, but often we see them balancing precariously from branches or shrubs. The sentries continuously turn their heads one way then the other, and scan the sky as well to make sure that no predators sneak up or dive from above, a behaviour that makes them look perpetually nervous.

The park has its share of creepy-crawlies – snakes, lizards, scorpions, and spiders galore. But the only one that bothers us is the African giant millipede, mostly black, thick as a big cigar, and reaching well over six inches long. They tend to come out late in the day when it's cooler, so driving back to camp is like negotiating a slalom course, trying to dodge the plump, juicy strands of black spaghetti. After a rain they emerge en masse. Our chalet at Nossob rest camp is at ground level. We like to keep the doors open to let in the cooler evening air, but it's an open invitation to these multi-legged monsters that can quickly wriggle under a bed or behind a fridge or cupboard.

It's not only millipedes that we have to dodge along the gravel and sand roads. Occasionally big stones work their way to the surface. Most roads are simply deep trenches dug into the sand, and while the park does maintain them, it's not that often. With heavy use, the sandy surfaces become extremely rough, usually with coarse corrugations that are enough to make your head rattle if you hit them too fast. Signs encourage drivers to deflate their tires, to both cut down on the corrugations and to give a smoother ride. One sign at a picnic site says, "Have you deflated your tyres? If not, don't complain about the roads!" The posted speed limit in the park is 60 km/hour, but along some stretches, if we hit anything over 30 km/hour, it feels like our car is about to disintegrate. Ironically, those rough corrugations would later save us.

We spend time at each of the three main rest camps on the South African side of the park. Each one has a combination of chalets and campgrounds with a surrounding fence to keep out wildlife. Nossob rest camp is powered by a generator, which is turned off during the night to conserve energy. Not only does this bring complete, pitch-black darkness, but it's so quiet that every little sound becomes amplified. One night we hear lions roaring just outside the fence, an unforgettable sound that sends shivers down your spine.

To have a chance of getting even closer to wildlife with little or nothing between us and the vast desert, it's hard to beat spending a few nights in an unfenced wilderness camp. The largest one in the park is Kalahari Tented Camp with a spectacular setting on the banks of the Auob River Valley. Our deck overlooks a waterhole in the distance where we watch wildebeest, jackals, foxes, and lions come to drink. One evening, just as the fading twilight makes it difficult to see, we spot tall, stick-like shapes shimmering in the distance. As they come closer, we make out about a dozen giraffes on their way to the waterhole. It's difficult and awkward for them to reach the water; they must first splay out their long front legs, then lower their heads to drink.

Our accommodation is technically a tent with canvas walls, but it sits on a slightly raised platform with a permanent and substantial wooden floor, and beds as good as in any hotel room. The units have an attached bathroom, and a kitchen in a separate side building just across the patio. Being totally self-contained, you don't have to go out at night, since animals could be anywhere. When we drive into our parking spot, we close a high gate behind us, but the front patio remains completely open to the world. We wake up before dawn each morning so that we can be out for sunrise. But before walking the five or six steps to the kitchen to make breakfast, we look around extremely carefully, shining the flashlight in every direction to see if any surprise guests happen to be lurking about. We only see ground squirrels and mongoose come by, but from time to time, guests report lions or hyenas right by the tents. Just before coming on this trip, we read a report by visitors who witnessed lions devouring a wildebeest right outside their tent.

Kielie Krankie wilderness camp is completely different, with only four rust-coloured cabins sitting atop the highest sand dune in the area, blending into the red sand. Here, more than anywhere, the expanse of desert in every direction gives us the feeling of really being "out there". Just as we're about to leave the next morning, the attendant runs out and calls us back to have a look. A brown hyena is drinking at a nearby waterhole that we can see clearly from our balcony. Restricted to the arid regions of southern Africa, the prehistoric-looking creature is covered in a thick coat of shaggy brown hair. The timing couldn't be better in the soft, early morning light. We had been hoping to photograph this fairly rare hyena, but the few times we caught a fleeting glimpse of this shy and elusive animal, we came up empty-handed – until today.

It doesn't rain a lot in the Kalahari, but when it does, it often comes along with dramatic thunderstorms. We see a lot of dry thunderstorms with billowing dark clouds and plenty of lightning, but no moisture. One evening, we sit outside and watch the light show for hours, with jagged streaks of light and sheet lightning brightening the sky and open landscape. Most intriguing is lightning that stays within a cloud, looking as if the entire cloud is on fire.

Then things change quickly. We're exploring about 20 kilometres out of Nossob rest camp on our afternoon drive. The sky is definitely more active than normal, with low and fast-moving black thunderclouds all around. We decide it's time to make our way back along the rough corrugated sand roads. Suddenly the skies open up with a vengeance, rain pounding so hard that the windshield wipers can't keep up. This isn't a passing storm; it keeps hammering us, water flooding the normally dry riverbed, and flowing to the lowest areas, including the road. Water pours into the road like floodgates had been opened, cutting right through the high sandy banks. Not only can we barely see because of the relentless rain, but the rushing water quickly turns the road into a flowing river. It's a no-win situation – we're afraid to stop and risk getting inundated or stuck, and afraid to keep going because we can't see what's ahead. Then we remember that before long, we'll be coming to a slight rise overlooking a waterhole in this mostly flat land. We'll try to make it that far, then decide what to do next.

We make it to the high ground, which looks like an island in an ever expanding lake. Before long, a four-wheel drive truck comes from behind and pulls up alongside. It's Andrew and Lucy, a couple from Johannesburg we had met from time to time in our travels around the park. We seriously discuss abandoning our small Toyota Corolla, getting a ride to camp with them, then coming back for the car the next day. But by now, the rain is subsiding somewhat, so we choose to go on, following closely behind their truck.

Although the rain lessens, the flow of water into the road becomes heavier. The flood waters easily breach lower sand banks lining the road, making it tough to judge where the edge of the road is. In the lowest stretches, we are literally pushing water, and the muddy spray splashes high over the top of the hood. We really start to worry when we see water coming up to the back bumper of that big truck. Staying immediately behind the truck proves to be a big help, since the truck pushes the water to the side and we drive in its wake.

Amazingly, we are able to keep moving, thanks in part to these rough roads. We're no longer cursing those bone-wrenching corrugations; they now provide just enough grip and traction to keep going. Any minute we expect the engine to stop, as the spark plugs and wiring are undoubtedly wet. Now our decision to keep moving instead of leaving the car on the high spot looks less and less like the right choice. If the car stalls, and is left sitting in deep water, things will get messy. We can imagine the questions at the car rental company ("You were driving where?"). Yet somehow, we make it back; the camp gates never looked so welcoming.

First we must check in at the camp office. Unlike other wildlife parks in South Africa, Kgalagadi has a visitor tracking system where you pick up your park permit before leaving the rest camp, telling them which direction you're heading. Then at the end of the day, you check in again so they know you've made it back safely. Today especially, it strikes us as an excellent system.

Later on we get together with Andrew and Lucy to relive the afternoon's adventure and celebrate our good fortune at making it through the flood. "A few times when I looked back, I could see the water coming over the bonnet," says Andrew. "The headlights would flicker on and off as they shorted out."

We're staying in a chalet, so we know we'll have a dry bed tonight. Not everyone is so lucky; many sites in the adjoining campground are flooded out. One tent is completely surrounded by a moat.

The next morning, we have a better look at our car. Surprisingly, water did not come through the well-sealed doors, but it did come up through the floor, leaving the floor mats sopping wet. We mop up what we can and rely on the desert heat to take care of the rest. In the heat of the day, no one leaves a car in the sun if there's shade available. So we become somewhat of a curiosity in the rest camp, parking our car in full sun with the doors wide open. It takes three days of this routine to finally dry everything out.

Most surprising is how rapidly and dramatically the desert is transformed. Plants appear out of nowhere. Grey-looking shrubs wilting in the heat turn green with vigour. Devil's thorn, a low creeping plant with showy yellow flowers, suddenly erupts everywhere, covering sandy slopes in carpets of lemon. Trumpet-shaped red flowers of devil's claw, tall pink cat's tail, and bouquet-like clusters of pinkish narine add to the blooming bounty. It seems fitting that some flowers have stormy names – thunderbolt, a tall plant with dark purple flowers; or black storm, its bright yellow blossoms looking like candles stuck in the sand. The extraordinary parade of colour is set against fiery red dunes and a deep blue sky.

We've come to the Kalahari for the big cats, which certainly haven't disappointed us. But what we'll remember most is the larger experience of wandering through this striking and unspoiled land; a place that can be enchanting, stunning, and savage. Above all, it's a land of surprises, where we find magnificent wildflower displays in pure sand, and experience our worst ever rainstorm in the middle of a desert.

Painted Sands and Lonely Lands
Ramblings Through Southern Namibia

Highway sign near Luderitz, Namibia.

Africa is home to over a billion people, with crowded cities and a rapidly growing population. Namibia, however, is a world apart. Covering roughly the same area as France and Britain combined, this expansive country in southwest Africa has only two million people, giving it not only one of the lowest population densities in Africa, but also one of the lowest in the world. Most Namibians live in the northern half of the country, but where we're heading in the south, people are few and far between. We shouldn't have to worry about crowds or traffic jams.

As we drive though the sparse countryside, it soon becomes apparent why there are so few people. Southern Namibia is the meeting ground for two of the world's great deserts – the Kalahari in the east that borders South Africa and Botswana, and the vast Namib Desert spreading far inland from the Atlantic coast. Yet this "empty" land is home to some of Africa's most magnificent sights.

We enter Namibia at a minor border crossing from the South African side of Kgalagadi Transfrontier Park in the Kalahari Desert. It's a half-day drive along lonely gravel roads to the town of Mariental, the nearest community with services such as supermarkets and banks. We spend the night at the campground at the edge of town, then next morning stock up on provisions for our visit to the Namib Desert.

The last order of business is to get some cash. Having just come from South Africa where bank machines worked without fail, we naively assume that this will be a simple routine matter. An ATM displays the familiar international symbols that presumably mean that our bank card will work. However, it won't even recognize our card. We usually travel with cards from at least three different banks, in each of our names, just in case something like this happens. We try all the other cards. Same story. Maybe a cash advance from Visa or MasterCard? We have credit cards from three different banks. Nope, absolutely nothing, even though we successfully used one of the credit cards at a supermarket earlier. Perhaps a different ATM? The same thing happens, or rather, doesn't happen. Mariental has three banks, and we come to a dead end at every one, with every bank card and every credit card.

Exhausting our options, there's no choice but to continue on and hope that we can solve the problem somewhere down the road. Not completely out of money, we still have some South African Rand, which is at par with the Namibian Dollar and accepted everywhere. But we'll have to ration our spending closely. Credit cards may be accepted at major businesses in urban areas, but once off-the-beaten-track, cash is essential. Fuel, food, and accommodation are now our spending priorities. Treats such as ice cream and beer may have to wait; quite a sacrifice in the scorching desert heat.

After a stretch of pavement, it's back to lonely gravel roads with little traffic, passing through a mix of arid and semi-arid landscapes that somehow support farms. A winding pass takes us through the Tsaris Mountains, with sandstone walls splashed in shades of purple and orange. Then it's a long descent toward the sandy land of the Namib Desert.

Stopping for fuel at a petrol station in the middle of the desert, we see an ATM inside, so decide it's at least worth a try. Once again, card after card leads to a dead end. Then on our last try – a Visa card – the machine starts spitting out cash. It's like hitting the jackpot on a casino slot machine! We celebrate with an ice cream, and buy some cold beer.

Our main destination is Sesriem, gateway to Namib-Naukluft National Park. Covering close to 50,000 square kilometres, it's among the largest parks in the world. We've always been enamoured with sand dunes, but these are undeniably the ultimate – one of those rare places that exceeds expectations by a long shot.

The oldest desert in the world also boasts the biggest dunes in the world, with some over 300 metres or close to 1,000 feet high. But what really stands out is the colour – oxidizing iron in the sand makes it a brilliant reddish-orange, but under different light conditions, shades can change from fire-engine red to a subtle pink to yellowy-beige. Before coming, we see lots of photos of these dunes, and can't help but wonder if the flamboyant colours are real. They are. For photographers, a visit to the Namib is like dying and going to heaven.

The ideal place to stay is Sesriem campsite, right at the park entrance gate. We're driving a small car, and the only time we get stuck throughout our sand-bound trip is right inside the campground. We're allocated a site on the far side, but half way there, our car becomes hopelessly hung up on a sand drift. It takes the help of people pushing back and forth to get us out. The park changes our site to one closer to the road, leaving the other site for visitors with four-wheel drive vehicles. Most of the spacious sites have a shady camelthorn tree, surrounded by a half-metre-high stone fence that helps keep out drifting sand.

From the park entrance the road runs for about 60 kilometres along a gradually narrowing valley with massive dunes on both sides. The route follows the bed of the Tsauchab River, although you would never know it. The ephemeral river only holds water when it rains heavily, and this is extremely rare. But the valley does have enough residual moisture to support a few grasses and shrubs, and even the occasional tree. Vegetation is also nourished by sea fogs that develop along the Atlantic coast and drift far inland.

Near the start of the road, we pass a mix of mountains and sand dunes. In one spot, sand almost completely covers a mountain, leaving only its sharp spires protruding on top. Soon after, the landscape transforms to almost pure sand. Every dune is unique, and is constantly being reshaped by the wind to produce crescents, hummocks, ridges, sharp edges, and blowouts. On the valley floor, the odd tree miraculously clings to life in the windswept, sand-clogged land. Not only do trees and plants struggle for moisture and endure scorching temperatures, but many wage a losing battle with shifting sand. We pass one tree that bends as the leading edge of a dune slowly but surely buries it, and we can't help but wonder how long it will be before it's totally swallowed by the migrating dune.

The appropriately named Dune 45, reached after travelling 45 kilometres, is considered the most photographed sand dune in the world. It isn't the tallest dune, but its convenient setting right beside the road, and relatively gradual slope, make it a favourite to climb. And there's no better place for sunrise. One morning we head out an hour before daybreak, keeping a close eye out for the inevitable springbok that graze near the road or wander across. Climbing to the top of the dune in the cool morning air gives us a good work-out; it's tough to make much headway when you keep sinking into loose deep sand. We're joined by a dozen or so other early-risers. As the sun clears the eastern horizon, it immediately floods the dune crests with the most intense reds, pinks, and oranges imaginable, contrasting with dark shadows between the slopes. Soon the entire valley becomes saturated in an orange-red glow.

It's more fun to take a shortcut to the bottom, running down the extremely steep slope. Unlike running down a hill, there's little chance of losing control, since we sink up to our ankles with every step. All too soon, the fun ends and we empty out our sand-clogged boots at the base of the towering dune. Months later, we still find those fine grains of red sand hiding under the insoles.

Gazing up at the top of the dune, we see the light changing. The sand stays vibrant orange, while the sky turns a brilliant blue. Of the gazillion or so photos we take, one is a simple close-up showing a piece of sand and a piece of the sky. A "rule" of composition says that you shouldn't put the horizon across the dead centre of a photo, but here the intensity of the orange and blue competed for attention. Two equal slices of orange and blue seemed to symbolize the essential nature of the Namib Desert – sand and sky. A year later, we're pleased to learn that this attempt at minimalist art was chosen as a finalist in the Creative Visions of Nature category in the Wildlife

Photographer of the Year competition, sponsored by the BBC and the British Museum of Natural History.

Another 15 kilometres past Dune 45, the road ends, as dunes on either side of the valley converge to form a funnel. About five kilometres beyond is Sossusvlei, which roughly means dead-end marsh or marsh of no return. Those with four-wheel drive vehicles and high clearance can make it, but for us this is not an option. Instead we climb aboard one of the four-wheel drive shuttles that run regularly between the parking lot at the end of the road and Sossusvlei.

We arrive just before sunrise in order to catch the magical morning light. Our driver weaves and zigzags through the thick sand trail, trying to keep up speed so as not to get bogged down in the sand. Fortunately he makes it, and drops us off at trail's end at Sossusvlei. The word vlei is Afrikaans for shallow depression or marsh, which once existed here when there was water. Any semblance of wetlands is long gone, and now monstrous sand dunes surround the bone dry pan. Looking at the lay of the land, we see the dead end, how the Tsauchab River was prevented from flowing. We're still over 60 kilometres from the Atlantic Ocean, with nothing between us and the ocean but an immense sea of sand.

These dunes are not only the biggest, but also the most attractive, flowing in broad sinuous curves with knife-edge crests, higher and higher, and blending into the vast dune fields beyond. The rising sun highlights the apricot-coloured dune peaks, contrasting with deep shadows in the troughs.

We walk about two kilometres to another famous pan that competes with Sossusvlei for the most spectacular setting. Dead Vlei is literally a dead marsh. Hundreds of years ago, the clay pan formed when the Tsauchab River flooded, allowing camelthorn trees to flourish. When the climate changed and the area dried, the trees died. It became so dry and scorched that they didn't decompose, but rather became desiccated where they stood in this barren tree graveyard. Thought to be around 900 years old, they appear black after being exposed to the searing sun for so many years. This alien landscape takes on an enchanting character of its own, with shimmering heat waves wafting across the brilliant white floor of the pan, contrasting with the stark black skeletons of ancient trees, all set against a backdrop of orange dunes.

While colours are most vibrant near sunrise and sunset, they change throughout the day. Our normal routine is to go out as soon as the park gate opens before sunrise, come back to camp to rest in the shade during the heat of the day, then head out again in mid-afternoon and stay out until sunset. One day we stay in the dunes until noon when the blazing sun turns the landscape into a gigantic blast furnace. Colours on the dunes shift to pastel shades of coral and peach. From a distance, we watch shimmering mirages form and change shape as the intense heat waves cause distortions and appear to melt away part of the scene.

The only part of the Tsauchab River to have permanent water is Sesriem Canyon, and even here there isn't much. About four kilometres from the campground, the canyon isn't apparent until we walk right up to it. The narrow fissure, up to 30 metres deep in places, reveals layers of easily eroded sandstone and sculpted rock formations. It was an important water source for early inhabitants and Afrikaner settlers. The name originated because it took six (*ses*) lengths of hide rope (*riem*) to draw out the water.

We're surprised at the amount of wildlife. While animals aren't abundant, it's amazing that this inhospitable, sand-filled land supports any at all. The most obvious are springbok, small antelope that have the dangerous habit of hanging around the edge of the road at dawn and dusk. The antelope most at home in the desert is the gemsbok, also known as oryx. A striking tan, chocolate, and white animal, they are famous for their mostly straight horns, close to one metre long and ending in razor-sharp points. They venture far into the dunes, and are able to cope with the intense heat because of specialized blood vessels that cool the blood. Where water isn't available, they'll dig for it underground or subsist on plants with a high moisture content.

Heading south of Sesriem, we travel roads that have even less traffic. It's not unusual to drive an hour and a half or more without meeting another vehicle. The first part of this route passes through the Namib Rand Nature Reserve, considered one of the largest private nature reserves in southern Africa. Surprisingly, almost all of it is fenced. Farm holdings are enormous, as they need to be. It looks like it would take several of these sparsely vegetated acres to feed each sheep.

Desert sands continue, but now we see more rocky hills and low mountains, and a thin cover of grass and other vegetation. The almost unreal colours range from brilliant red sand, to rusty tinged mountains, all set against a clear blue sky. Most intriguing is the colour of the road, which abruptly changes from white to pink to cinnamon. The sudden change has to do with the gravel spread on the road; gravel from the pink pit goes so far, then the white gravel takes over.

In this isolated land of shifting sands and arid mountains, the last thing we expect to find is a German castle. But there it is, a genuine castle complete with fortified battlements and turrets, sitting in a remote corner of the African bush. Baron Hans Heinrich von Wolf began building the 22-room castle called Dusiwib in 1908.

Blocks of reddish-purple sandstone were quarried in nearby hills, while stonemasons brought from various parts of Europe put it all together. The rest of the material and furnishings were imported from Germany. The attached farm raised prize stud horses.

The German aristocrat and his wife lived here only five years. The baron was visiting Germany on a horse-buying trip when World War I broke out. He joined the army and was killed in battle in France. His wife had no interest in returning to the Namibian desert, so the extravagant castle was abandoned. Eventually it was taken over by the government and restored as an historic site.

We stop to camp at Lovedale Farm, which as a sideline to its livestock operation, offers travellers' accommodation and campsites. It's quite a revelation how old and new technology work together on this isolated sheep farm. On our arrival, the lady running the place tells us that the water should be hot enough for a shower in an hour or so. She lights a small fire in an outdoor contraption called a "donkey", something that has been used on African farms since the early settler days. Although there's only a few sticks on the fire, the boiler and series of pipes it heats gives us plenty of hot water. They have adopted solar energy in a big way, something that makes sense in this country where the sun almost always shines. A diesel powered generator has long been a staple in this remote location far off the electricity grid, but now they run the generator for less than an hour a day, with solar power providing the rest.

Arriving at the paved B4 Highway, we turn west toward the coastal city of Luderitz. The mountainous terrain levels out and is replaced by an endless desert of white sand where the straight road disappears into a distant horizon. Driving major highways in Namibia, we occasionally pass picnic sites on the side of the road, usually something very simple like a cement table and a couple seats under a shady tree. But here we find what is undoubtedly the world's loneliest picnic spot – a cement table with a single cement stool, along with one scrawny green shrub less than a metre tall. In every direction the landscape is wide open, broken only by the long straight black ribbon of highway. Despite the searing heat and blasting desert winds, we feel compelled to stop at this incongruous spot.

Closer to Luderitz, the highway leaves the high flat desert and starts winding down toward the sea. Signs warn of blowing sand, and bulldozers busily scrape away drifts that accumulate on the road. It's amazing how fast the sand can take over in even a moderate wind. We're reminded of snow drifts that accumulate on winter roads, but sand is much more dangerous than snow, and hitting even a small sand drift could overturn a car.

Luderitz is a strange city in a strange setting – windswept and perched on inhospitable rocky hills mostly devoid of vegetation. Its reason for being is a seaport in a protected harbour, the only ship-friendly place along this wild stretch of the Atlantic coast. In the 1880s, it was the point of entry for Germany establishing the colony of South West Africa. With Germany's defeat in World War I, South Africa administered South West Africa under a mandate from the League of Nations, an arrangement intended to be temporary. In effect, the territory became a colony of South Africa, which refused to give up control even after the United Nations declared its continued occupation illegal. This led to a prolonged war of independence that lasted until the late 1980s. Namibia eventually became independent in 1990. Luderitz's importance as a port decreased as most shipping moved farther north up the coast to the deeper harbour at Walvis Bay.

One claim to fame that Luderitz still retains is its reputation for ferocious winds. We're buffeted by howling gales everywhere we go, especially near the water where choppy waves with spray blowing off the white caps fill the "protected harbour". We take a drive just outside town along the Luderitz Peninsula. The route promises coastal scenery, sea bird colonies, fur seals, and an historic spot where Bartholomew Diaz planted a cross in 1488. The Portuguese explorer stopped here on the return leg of his epic journey, becoming the first European to round the Cape of Good Hope on the southern end of Africa.

The rough road of sand and rock takes us to Diaz Point where a lighthouse and reconstructed historic cross sit on a point jutting into the Atlantic. The setting is ruggedly beautiful, but the unrelenting wind on this exposed coast makes it difficult to even walk upright to the base of the cross. Visibility is deteriorating in the blowing sand, so we decide to scrap the rest of the drive and head back to town. Stopping for fuel at a petrol station, we mention the winds to the attendant.

"This is nothing," he says, laughing. "If you can still stand up, we don't call it windy at all!"

Not all visitors complain about the wind. Windsurfers love it, and consider this among the best spots in the world to hone their skills. The annual Luderitz Speed Challenge is an international competition producing several world windsurfing speed records – more than 90 km/hour.

With around 15,000 people, Luderitz is the largest community we visit in southern Namibia. It's a pleasant enough place to spend a couple days, despite the wind. The city centre has several restored German colonial buildings, many painted vibrant shades of red, orange, yellow, and blue – welcome splashes of colour against the stark landscape. We check into the Luderitz Backpackers Lodge, a sprawling old house that could hold several travellers, but there's only one other couple staying there, coincidentally also from Canada. We spend an agreeable evening swapping travel stories with Nick and Joanne, who are in the early days of an ambitious trip driving from Cape Town to Europe. Finding a bank with an ATM that accepts our bank cards without problem undoubtedly bolsters our good mood.

About 10 kilometres outside Luderitz stands the bizarre ghost town of Kolmanskop. We had planned to stop here, but having been to plenty of ghost towns before, we assumed that it would be of only passing interest. Instead, it turns out to be among the most compelling spots along the trip.

Kolmanskop was the key to Luderitz's prosperity and indeed to Namibia's economy. In 1908, a railway worker noticed a shiny stone lying on the ground. A diamond. The rush was soon on to the richest diamond fields in the world. In the early years, "mining" consisted of workers crawling along the sand on their bellies, picking out the diamonds. The town boomed, with instant millionaires building elaborate mansions, many with ornate German colonial architecture. The prosperous town had every convenience, including its own railway tram. One thing it didn't have was good drinking water, but since no expense was spared, shipping water all the way from Cape Town easily solved the problem. Kolmanskop boasted the first x-ray machine in southern Africa. While handy for diagnosing broken bones and such, its main purpose was to catch workers who had swallowed diamonds. Eventually, the boom went bust. Shortly after World War I, the area was becoming depleted of diamonds while richer deposits were found farther south. Kolmanskop went into decline, and by the 1950s, the town was abandoned.

Some buildings at the historic site have been restored and maintained, providing a fascinating glimpse into a bygone era of wealth and extravagance. The most intriguing exhibit shows the many imaginative ways that workers tried but failed to smuggle out diamonds. The constantly drifting sand was kept at bay during Kolmanskop's heyday, but the sand is once again consuming all but a few restored buildings. Walking past building after building, we peer in through windows and doors at the eerie sight of sand dunes inside houses. Some drifts stand knee deep, while others reach almost to the ceiling and pour through adjoining doorways. Houses still have brightly painted or wallpapered walls, but instead of furniture, they're filled with perfectly formed dunes that are slowly but surely smothering the buildings inside and out.

The area surrounding Kolmanskop and Luderitz is part of the Sperrgebiet, or forbidden zone, a sprawling desert region originally set aside by the Germans that is still claimed and protected for diamond exploration. Being right in the midst of diamond country, and knowing that the ground cover constantly shifts, you can't help but wonder if you'll just come across a diamond somewhere.

"Hope that never happens," warns the guide taking visitors around Kolmanskop. "One of the most serious crimes in Namibia is the illegal possession of diamonds."

The town of Aus sits beside the long highway running east from Luderitz. We spend the night at a nearby campground, off by itself in rugged desert terrain, surrounded by high rocky hills. Our site is on the far edge of the campground, so it's almost like being completely alone in the desert. A sprawling camelthorn tree provides welcome shade, not only for us, but also for a colony of birds occupying a gargantuan nest about two metres across that's suspended in the branches above us.

Sparrow-sized sociable weavers build the largest communal nest of any bird in the world. Found only in arid parts of southern Africa, these insect-eating, buff-brown birds cooperate in creating nest complexes that can house up to a hundred birds. Made of grass, the nests look like haystacks stuck up in a tree. Always on the move, the small birds constantly chatter as they fly back and forth bringing strands of grass to shore up the nest. While it's nice to be able to watch the comings and goings at this nest at such close quarters, we can't help but think that they attract cobras that, once inside, find a tasty bird buffet.

With the last rays of sunshine, the rocky hills turn scarlet, then come nightfall, the darkness is complete, accentuating countless stars in the clear desert sky. In true desert fashion, the intense heat turns to cold in a matter of a couple hours.

Not far from Aus roam the legendary wild horses of the Namib Desert. They've been around for over a hundred years, almost ghostlike and seldom seen. No one is sure where they came from. Theories on their origin range from transport ships that ran aground on the coast, to escapees from farms, to military horses being released after they were no longer needed. Another legend is that they came from the horse stud farm at Dusiwib Castle. Somehow, this herd has learned to survive in one of the mostly unlikely horse habitats imaginable, with only sparse grass, little water, and punishing summer heat. One adaptation is that they often eat their own dung, which provides part of the nutrients they need. In recent years, they've tended to hang out in an area just north of the highway, so a well was dug here to provide a reliable water source. We take the short detour to the waterhole just in case they happen to be there, and hit it lucky. Several horses finish drinking and shortly after wander back into the grassless barren hills.

Keetmanshoop is a town at the crossroads of the highway to Luderitz and the main north-south highway running between South Africa and Namibia's capital, Windhoek. We're here to see the famed Quiver Tree Forest, a short drive away. The strange yet majestic quiver tree has a limited range, found only in southern Namibia and the far northwestern part of South Africa. Growing up to nine metres tall with a thick, straight barrel-like trunk, it isn't really a tree, but rather a huge aloe plant. The name came from San Bushmen who hollowed out its branches to make quivers for their arrows.

These trees dot the landscape throughout the region, usually standing by themselves in arid rocky terrain. But on a section of a farm that's been turned into a nature preserve, they grow in profusion in a forest-like grouping. The best part is that there's a campground right beside the forest, making it easy to photograph at both sunset and sunrise without even leaving camp. The reserve is another photographer's dream where we catch the colour of the sky shining through the symmetrical half-dome of branches starting about two-thirds the way up the trunk.

A short drive down the road brings us to the other-worldly Giant's Playground. Through eons of weathering and other natural forces, mammoth dolerite boulders have been left in formations that, at first glance, look man-made. It's as if a giant has been playing around with oversized Lego blocks, creating structures that can reach up to three stories high. In places, the boulders are so closely fitted together that they're like the ancient Inca walls of South America. In others, it's as if someone has tried to see how many blocks could be piled one on top of the other, or haphazardly placed rusty-red rocks in crooked piles that are about to collapse. We can't help but be drawn in to see what bizarre surprises hide around the next rocky corner. But then the trail peters out, and with formations looking remarkably alike, we lose our way in the jumbly maze; it takes us a while to get our bearings and eventually pick up the main trail again.

Heading south to the Fish River Canyon, the shortest route is along a gravel road that appears in reasonable condition, until we come to a dry river bed crossing. A grader that had been working on the crossing now sits hopelessly stuck in the soft gravel, its wheels half buried. Nearby, the driver waits in the shade for help to arrive. Two other vehicles are stopped ahead of us. The drivers walk over the stony gravel to see if they can find a safe way through, and since they both have four-wheel drive, decide to give it a go. It's obvious that our small car doesn't have a chance, so we have no choice but to backtrack to Keetmanshoop and take the long way around, adding another couple hours to the drive.

The Fish River Canyon is a land of superlatives. Various claims are bandied about – the largest canyon in Africa, or the second largest in the world, but rankings are always difficult because they depend on how measurements are made. There's no doubt that it's big. Really big. The Fish is Namibia's longest river, winding 650 kilometres from the Naukluft Mountains, flowing south into the Orange River that forms the border between Namibia and South Africa. For over 150 kilometres of its length, the river has formed a spectacular gouge in the earth, well over a half kilometre deep in places.

The view is sudden and dramatic. The terrain is mostly flat plateau until we approach the rim, then it's as if the earth simply falls away. Below us stretches an immense canyon carved and shaped by the power of the twisting river. We hike along the rim to various vantage points, walking between sparse clumps of grass and cactus that somehow manage to eke out a living in this parched terrain. While it is possible to drive some of the rough trails, in many places the "road" is simply a track over jumbles of rocks. The stones are so sharp and jagged that we have visions of being stranded as our tires are shredded to bits.

We stay at Hobas campground, about 10 kilometres from the rim. The pleasant spot has some of the few shade trees in the area. The only problem is baboon raiding parties, where groups of these noisy primates move through, grabbing anything that resembles food. They're constantly rummaging in the garbage cans, turning them over and making a terrible mess. One campground attendant spends half his time trying to chase them away, but they don't scare easily. It's been drier than normal, he tells us, so the baboons have fewer food options. He cautions us to not even turn around while cooking, or our supper could quickly disappear.

There's a challenging multi-day hike of about 85 kilometres through the canyon, but in summer (when we're there) the park closes the trail because the intense heat deep in the canyon makes it too dangerous for hiking. Temperatures topping 40 degrees Celsius are common and it can get close to 50 degrees.

So we do the next best thing and take the rough road that heads to the south end of the canyon at Ai-Ais, which means burning water in the local Nama language. This oasis-like spot is home to a hot springs resort where the sulphurous water is said to cure all manner of ailments. Gradually we wind our way down from the rim toward the canyon floor, more or less paralleling the hiking trail. It's one incredible view after another – orange rocky mountains framing the canyon slopes, quiver trees growing in pure sand and rock, multi-hued strands in the mountain cliffs varying from red to maroon to purple.

It seems fitting that our last stop in Namibia doesn't fail to serve up yet another surprising visual treat. It's not always easy to summarize impressions of a place, but for southern Namibia, one word stands out. Colour.

Butterscotch Pudding with Whipped Cream
Saskatchewan's Athabasca Sand Dunes

Giant dune, Athabasca Sand Dunes.

We're travelling a narrow ribbon between two vastly different worlds. The east bank of the river is clothed in dark green jackpine forest typical of northern Saskatchewan. But on the west side, all we see is massive banks of golden sand, in places rising more than 30 metres straight out of the water. When we pull our canoe into shore and struggle to the top of the banks, the sand stretches west as far as we can see. We're overlooking the largest sand dunes in Canada, and the largest this far north anywhere in the world.

We've returned to one of our favourite places on Earth – the William River flowing through the Athabasca Sand Dunes. Of all the spectacular landscapes we have visited around the world, Athabasca remains the most special for us. It was our earlier travels here that were responsible for a major shift in our lives, leading to a career in book publishing.

During our first trip to the dunes, we were on assignment for *Canadian Geographic* magazine to write an article on this mostly unknown and little-visited landscape. Most of our travel writing and photography until then had been geared toward magazines and newspapers, but we were so taken with Athabasca that we were convinced that articles were not enough. These fascinating dunes needed an entire book. So after a few return visits to explore further and round out our photography, we published our first book – *Northern Sandscapes – Exploring Saskatchewan's Athabasca Sand Dunes.* It turned out that the timing was right for the book. The Saskatchewan government had just completed extensive scientific studies on the dunes, then protected the area in a new provincial park. People were curious to see what all the fuss was about.

These are among the most unusual of the world's great dune fields. As we might expect, the biggest sand dunes are normally found in deserts or at least in dry climates. But not here. It's as if a chunk of a desert-like terrain had been picked up and plopped right in the middle of northern Canada's boreal forest and lakelands. The dunes border the ninth largest lake in North America, the fourth largest lake entirely within the borders of Canada. Three rivers slice right through the dune fields, something we don't expect to find in either northern forest or sand dunes. It's this surprising though delightful mix of sand, water, and trees that makes these dunes spellbinding.

The Athabasca Sand Dunes are practically in our back yard, about 800 kilometres north of our home in Saskatoon. Yet, this is one of the more difficult places to reach. It's actually more straightforward to travel to the dunes in the Namibian desert on the other side of the globe; fly to Namibia or South Africa, rent a car, and simply drive to the park. The Athabasca Sand Dunes have no road access, which is fortunate because the lack of easy access is helping to preserve this fragile landscape. On the other hand, it's quite challenging to visit. Once you arrive, there are absolutely no facilities of any kind – no scheduled transport, no shops, no accommodation or campgrounds, no buildings, no people, no cell service. Our kind of place.

The only options are to fly in or go by boat, and even these aren't easy. Stony Rapids is the only community on Lake Athabasca with road access, and that's a long, rough bone-jarring journey. Stony Rapids is at the extreme east end of Lake Athabasca, while the main dune fields are close to 200 kilometres farther west. It is possible to travel by boat from communities on Lake Athabasca, but crossing this expansive lake is like travelling on an inland sea, where huge waves are often the rule. The south shore along the dunes is also wide open, with no islands, no deep bays, and nowhere to hide in a storm or big waves. Motor boats have a tough time landing on the shallow, sand-choked shore. Depending on water levels, sandbars often extend far out from the lakeshore. And there's been accidents. A landmark on the beach in Thomson Bay is an old rusting tank, a remnant from a barge that broke up in a storm many years ago. Float planes can land on the water and drift in to shore, but only if the winds and water are calm enough. That's a big "if".

The first time we came here was by canoe, travelling down the William River. We drove to the end of the road in northwest

Saskatchewan, which ends on a rough mining exploration road at Carswell Lake. We paddled to the northern reaches of Carswell Lake, then made a short portage into the north-flowing Carswell River. Several times we ran aground on this extremely shallow river, and had no choice but to pick up our gear and carry it to deeper water. Things changed when the Carswell emptied into the much bigger William River. There's more water, but also more rocks and rapids. Our main memory of that trip was of one big rock garden, where we were constantly dodging boulders and picking our way through rocky rapids.

We knew we were getting close to the dunes, but when we rounded a bend and saw them for the first time, it still came as a surprise – a golden wall of sand lining the west bank. That dune stands all by itself, as if stranded away from the main dune field. After a short paddle, we hit the widespread William River Dune Field. For the next 25 kilometres, we travelled along this strange narrow ribbon, with familiar forest on the east bank, and gigantic walls of sand on the west.

Never have we seen a river change its character so completely as the William. For most of its course, this stony river is defined by rocks, rocks, and more rocks. About 18 kilometres before the river's end, there's one last flourish of frothing rapids plunging over rocky shelves, framed by car-sized boulders. Then suddenly it's as if we emerge into an entirely different river. The sand takes over, choking the river and spreading it into a wide braided stream, up to a half kilometre wide in places. There isn't a rock in sight, hardly even a tiny pebble. It stays like this all the way to Lake Athabasca.

It becomes even wider as the sand-choked delta of the William fans into Lake Athabasca, with a myriad of shallow channels shooting sand far into the lake. Sandbars are everywhere, mixed with low islands where vegetation has taken hold in the semi-stabilized sand. On our first trip, we canoed, or rather tried to canoe, through the main delta. The water got so shallow that eventually we had to forget about paddling and walked, trying to keep the canoe afloat in water only inches deep. It felt peculiar walking far into that immense lake in ankle-deep water. Fortunately, the lake was uncharacteristically calm.

This time, we're planning on canoeing upstream on the William River as far as the end of the rapids, a trip we have done three other times over the years. Our pilot Cliff Blackmur from Athabasca Fishing Lodges flies us in his Single Otter float plane over the lower stretches of the river then circles the delta. We look down at one of the most remarkable sights anywhere. The William River is full of surprises, but saves its grand finale for those who fly over the braided section, which now magically becomes a gigantic abstract painting. Multi-hued shades of gold, beige, and copper reveal varying depths of underwater sandbars, while above water sandbars appear alabaster white, and deeper channels are chocolate brown. The overall effect of the swirling colours looks like butterscotch pudding marbled with whipped cream.

Cliff brings the float plane down near the mouth of a narrow creek that branches off the William River just before the delta. But even this smaller waterway spews an amazing amount of sand into the lake, forming its own delta just around the point from the main delta. We land well over a half kilometre from shore in water that is barely a foot deep. Cliff is concerned that the plane might drift into the sandbars and become stuck, so we waste no time untying the canoe from the pontoons of the plane and throwing in our gear. As we paddle away, Cliff immediately starts the plane and quickly gets airborne. As with most canoe trips we have taken in the north, we consider this the real start of the journey – when the pilot leaves and we're completely on our own in the wilderness.

Paddling upstream in a strong current is challenging at the best of times, but in these shallow conditions our paddles often hit ground and we have a hard time getting enough power. A trick for paddling in shallow water is to "pole", pushing on the river bottom with your paddle. But here, the unstable sandy bottom is forever moving, up to 10 metres a day scientists tell us, so usually it's like pushing into mush. Our progress is slow; many times a promising-looking channel simply ends, and we run aground. We're only travelling 18 kilometres upstream, but in reality it's a lot more than that since we continually zigzag across the wide river, trying to stay in the deeper channels.

After a day and a half of steady paddling, we reach the end of the rapids. This is our favourite spot in the entire dunes. Sand banks lining the west side are met by a tongue of sand on the east bank from the extensive Thomson Bay Dune Field that stretches all the way to the lake. At this spot, the dune fields come together, almost overwhelming the river that separates them.

The partially damp dune slacks just back of the west bank are ideal for many rare plants. Protecting the unique plant life of the Athabasca Sand Dunes was a principal reason for establishing the provincial park. In fact, botanists consider this among the most important places in Canada for the study of rare plants. Over 50 species are considered rare, and some are endemic, growing nowhere else on Earth. When the park was created, 10 endemics had been identified. More recently, the number most often used is eight, since a very small number of a couple plants have tentatively been identified in other places. In any event, these are extremely rare plants.

The features of some are so esoteric that only botanists could get excited, but many are obvious to even a casual observer. Among the most widespread is the felt-leaved willow, with fuzzy bluish-green leaves that have the look and feel of felt. Sand chickweed is a low growing plant with delicate, minuscule white flowers at the end of thin stems. Yet this fragile-looking plant is so tough that it seems to thrive in pure sand. The most intriguing is the Athabasca thrift. Recognized by its distinctive round head with a cluster of little pink flowers sitting atop a long stem, it's like a miniature candy apple stuck in the sand.

It's not only rare plants that make this region so special. Early in the summer, the sand is carpeted in yellow with blooming sand heather. We find bright pink stemless ladyslippers in various parts of the north, but nothing like here. In some forested areas bordering the dunes, the ladyslippers are so thick that it's difficult to walk between them. On our way up the river, we stop at a willow-covered island for lunch. The sandy ground appears to have a reddish tinge, and when we look closer, we find thousands of oblong-leaved and round-leaved sundews that derive nutrients from absorbing insects trapped in sticky dew on hairs projecting from their leaves. A common though bizarre sight is exposed tree roots that are up to three metres above ground; over the years winds have blown away the supporting sand, undermining many trees.

The end of the rapids is also the perfect jumping-off point to visit Athabasca's magnificent giant dunes. The William River Dune Field is about 15 kilometres across. Near the centre stand 40 or so giant dunes, some over a kilometre long and 35 metres high. They aren't visible from the river. All we can see is an endless expanse of sand, gradually rising toward the horizon. It takes a couple hours to walk to these dunes. As we start out it's a bit disconcerting heading into a sea of sand. After a half hour or so, we gain enough altitude to see the monsters looming in the distance. While the direct distance to the first big dune is only about five kilometres or so, it takes so long because we have to weave a circuitous route around the expanses of desert pavement, the most fragile feature of the dunes. The wind has winnowed away the top layer of sand, leaving slightly heavier pebbles sitting on top. If we were to step on this formation, our footprints would be visible for years.

We take our time wandering along the edges of the desert pavement looking for ventifacts, strange Brazil-nut shaped stones that have been sandblasted for thousands of years. While sandblasted rocks are not unusual, what's peculiar about these is that they have been blasted from two different sides. Prevailing winds come from the northwest today, but the speculation is that winds came from a different direction thousands of years ago, accounting for the rocks' sharp angular formation. When researching our *Northern Sandscapes* book, we talked to two German scientists who had studied ventifacts throughout the world. They said that those of Athabasca were the most well defined specimens they had come across anywhere.

It is only practical to hike to the giant dunes in relatively calm weather. More than once, we have started out from the river, only to be forced to turn back when winds whipped the sand and filled the air. Blowing sand can make short work of camera gear in these conditions. It's not so great for our eyes either, and our exposed skin soon feels like coarse sandpaper. We usually set out on the hike in early evening since there's a better chance that winds will abate later in the day. Plus there's the added bonus of enjoying sunset on the big dunes, which comes around 10:30 in mid-summer – an unforgettable highlight of this unique area.

We notice a variety of animal and bird tracks on the dunes

just back of the river. But less than 500 metres into the dune field, the tracks disappear. The only sign of birdlife is a few Arctic terns, which sometimes nest on the desert pavement. They watch us carefully, screaming and scolding us for passing through their territory. This area marks the southern reaches of their nesting range in mainland Canada.

Plantlife thins out very quickly as we move farther into the dune field, but even around the big dunes, clumps of sea lyme grass dot the landscape. This tall robust grass normally grows in maritime areas of Canada. It is rare in Saskatchewan, except in the dunes, where we see it almost everywhere.

From a distance, the dunes appear long and undulating, like humpback whales in a sea of sand. When we arrive at one of the larger ones, it rises straight up from the level floor of the dune field. Strong winds from both east and west have sculpted the dunes, creating curving knife-edge crests. The sand feels reasonably solid as we walk along the level dune field, but as soon as we start climbing, we struggle and sink ankle deep with every step. Near the top, the dune becomes increasingly sharp, with a gradual slope to the west and a more precipitous drop to the east.

Sitting on top, we look over a series of other dunes stretching to the northwest, while to the north lies Lake Athabasca, and in the east we see a faint green line marking the east bank of the William River valley. As the low sun gradually dips in the west, the dune is transformed. The eastern side is thrown into deep shadow, while the sun-facing west slope turns from sandy yellow to rich shades of gold, then right at sunset it's painted with tinges of red.

Since we're almost always surrounded by sand, it's easy to see what critters have been wandering around. Tracks cover the beaches and dunes, giving the impression that wildlife is abundant. Moose, bear, caribou, wolf, rabbits, and a wide array of birds all leave their calling cards. Some of the most extensive networks of tracks belong to the Canadian toad, which wanders across the sand looking for tasty insects.

Seeing tracks is easy, but coming across the animals that made them is another matter. We have only seen a wolf once in the dunes, although we always see plenty of tracks. They go out of their way to avoid us. One morning we followed fresh wolf tracks that came along the water right toward our tent. Once the wolf had climbed the ridge to where our tent was visible, it suddenly changed direction, making a wide circle around our camp before continuing on.

One evening we hear sudden running behind our William River camp, then splashing in the river. It's a woodland caribou, running through the shallow water and across the low sandbars, apparently in an attempt to escape the clouds of mosquitoes. It finds a sandbar in the middle of the wide river and lies down for a welcome rest. Next day we see another caribou, as well as tracks in the sand showing that one has a young calf. These are thrilling though rare sightings. This iconic animal, portrayed on Canada's 25-cent piece, is quickly vanishing across Canada's boreal forest. Officially listed as "threatened", the woodland caribou is in serious danger of disappearing due to loss of habitat and increasing industrial development.

This is prime black bear country. They have wandered into our camps, but usually if we make enough noise, they will quickly move on. We know plenty are around because we see their tracks everywhere. One time while camping near the shore of Lake Athabasca, strong waves pounded the shore throughout the night, making it difficult to hear anything else. Next morning, we found fresh bear tracks right outside the tent. The bear was obviously curious enough to nose around, but fortunately didn't bother us. The only time we had serious concerns was at a sandbar campsite beside the William River. While eating supper, we glanced up to find the biggest black bear we have ever seen come out of the bush and walk straight toward us. We managed to scare it back into the forest, but it went slowly and reluctantly, as if to say "Okay, I'll go...for now." Right after supper, we packed up and moved our camp farther downriver.

The oddest bear encounter was also on the William. We were paddling downstream on the wide braided section, trying to stay in deep enough water in a fairly narrow channel. Just ahead, a bear came out of the thick bush on shore and started swimming across the river, without checking for traffic. We were headed straight for it. If we tried to veer off, we would likely get hung up on a shallow sandbar next to a surprised bear. On the other hand, running into a bear didn't seem too smart either. Just before we had to decide what to do, the swimming bear glanced our way. Its eyes practically popped out of its head as it did a quick flip and in a flash swam back to shore as we glided past.

The only critter to ever cause us problems was one moose. We encounter a lot of moose in our northern travels. If they see us at a distance, they may cautiously continue feeding, while keeping an eye on us. But if we're too close, almost every time moose will immediately flee. On our most recent trip, an adult moose and calf ran right beside our tent early one morning. Likely they were walking along, caught sight of our tent, then realized that something was out of the ordinary and decided to hightail it.

Things don't always go according to plan. One time we paddled downstream on the narrow creek that runs off the William River. The current was so strong that we simply had to steer along the twisting waterway. We rounded a sharp bend and suddenly came face to face with a big bull moose standing in the water. Not making any noise, we had surprised it. Instead of fleeing as most moose would do, he charged us. We looked up at his long legs splashing through the shallow water, his head down and aimed at the centre of the canoe. He hesitated for a split second and was almost on top of us. Robin swung his paddle and we heard a loud crack as the paddle caught the moose squarely on the end of his nose. The moose stopped just long enough to shake his head and try to figure out what to do next, while we paddled like mad to put some distance between us and the bad-tempered moose.

We're about to travel that same stretch again, as we leave our idyllic sandbar camp spot near the end of the rapids and head down river. The same section that was such a struggle to paddle upstream a few days earlier now takes us on a fast downstream joyride. Fortunately, this time we don't meet any cantankerous moose. Winds are picking up, and closer to the delta we can see waves crashing on the shore. There's no choice but to wait it out. The narrow creek is lined in thick bushy willows and shrubs, somewhat reminiscent of an impenetrable tropical stream. Near the mouth we find a section of level, semi-open jackpine forest right next to the water, the perfect spot to set up camp. We might as well settle in, since winds continue to howl away well into the evening.

We wake up at 4:00 the next morning with the intention of travelling to our favourite camping spot in Thomson Bay before the winds and waves arrive. As a general rule, winds are calmer in evening and early morning, but we've had enough experience with this lake to know that it plays by its own rules, doing what it likes when it likes. But this time we're lucky to paddle into the lake in near dead calm conditions. We've had forest fire smoke over the past few days, some from nearby fires and some drifting in from hundreds of kilometres away. With no wind, the smoke blankets the water like a shroud. Visibility is fine along the shore, but looking into the lake, the smoke partially obscures the rising sun, while the horizon disappears as the water and sky meld into a surreal steely grey.

We're struck by how dramatically different Lake Athabasca's south shore is from the north shore. The north is classic Precambrian Shield country, with rocky outcroppings, high granite cliffs, a labyrinth of islands, and deep bays. Some of the bays are so big that they are more like separate lakes. We've travelled much of the north shore by motor boat. Waves and storms can batter this shoreline as well, but we can usually find somewhere sheltered to wait it out.

While the south shore has nowhere to hide to escape nature's fury, we feel safer here in a canoe than in a motor boat. We're able to negotiate the extremely shallow water near shore. With the exception of a few stretches, non-stop beaches line the 100 kilometres or so of lakeshore in the sand dunes section. So when things get dicey, as they inevitably do, we can quickly pull into shore, drag the canoe up, and wait it out, sometimes for an hour or two, sometimes for several days. On one trip, we were stuck in the same spot for close to a week as relentless winds and pounding waves kept up day after day. Even after the winds calmed down, the momentum of the waves continued for an incredibly long time.

Our favourite spot along the south shore is the exhumed forest of Thomson Bay. Several ancient tree trunks, perhaps centuries old, stick out of the pure sandy slope overlooking the bay. It was a normal forest at one time, but was buried by sand as the dunes continued their steady eastward migration with the prevailing winds. Many years later, the winds pushed the sand even farther east, and began uncovering the age-old trees which have been desiccated, looking like petrified wood. Scattered among the remnants of still upright tree trunks are overturned dried roots, many resembling mythical sea serpents with octopus-like tentacles.

Fascinating at any time of day, in evening it becomes an enchanted forest. In mid-summer, the sun sets over the widest part of Lake Athabasca, dipping into the water with no land in sight. As it hangs over the great lake, the low sun shines slightly up toward the exhumed forest, bathing everything in a radiant glow. The ghostly sentinels take on a new character, their bare wooden shapes turning almost blood red with the sun's last rays.

According to a local Dene legend, this was once the land of giants. A giant hunter once threw a spear at a giant beaver that had built a huge dam on Lake Athabasca. Thinking he had killed the beaver, he tossed it onto the south shore of the lake. But the beaver wasn't quite dead, and it thrashed around to such an extent that the shore was ground into sand. Scientists tell us less colourful stories – about glaciers retreating some 9,000 years ago, and meltwater flowing through spillways such as the William River, depositing sandstone sediment in a delta in Glacial Lake Athabasca. As the lake receded and the land rebounded after the weight of the glacial ice was gone, the sand was exposed and whipped into dunes by strong winds.

Sweeping in a 25-kilometre arc just east of the William River delta, Thomson Bay has the largest dune field bordering the lake. But there are a lot more. Another 60 kilometres or so to the east, the Archibald River flows into Lake Athabasca after cutting through forest and sand. The effect is similar to that of the William River, with the east bank clothed in forest and the west bank covered in sand. The narrow river almost becomes lost, sandwiched between towering dunes and tall trees.

The eastern end of the dunes is marked by the MacFarlane River, the biggest and longest river in the park, bringing 11,000 tonnes of sand per day into the lake. This is a wild whitewater river for most of its length, with the last rapids ending about seven kilometres from the mouth. We're able to paddle upstream that far, first along the twisting meanders near the delta, then beside dunes lining the water for a short distance, and eventually to where the river spreads into a picturesque lake about two kilometres across. We're treated to yet another "room with a view" as we camp on a ridge overlooking forested hills, sand dunes, sandstone cliffs, and fingers of rapids spreading around willowy islands.

When Cliff first flew us into this area, he took us over a set of three beautiful waterfalls upstream from the little lake. Now we're anxious to see them up close. We decide to hike there, but the route isn't direct because of boggy terrain and canyons next to the water's edge. It's necessary to go back to the forested ridge overlooking the valley. Forest fires burned much of this area over the years, leaving a maze of deadfall looking like a jumble of pick-up sticks, with new growth so thick that it's often difficult to get through. Our all-day hike turns out to be a tough slog, but when we arrive at the falls, it all seems worthwhile. Framed by thick forest, boulders, and jagged bedrock, the river drops over a series of ledges of varying heights, forming a complex of picture-perfect cataracts rather than a single drop. Above all, it's a rare privilege to be in a place that very few people have ever visited.

So far at least, isolation has kept this special corner of the globe mostly intact. But these days, isolation can be fleeting. Lake Athabasca is downstream from the expansive and controversial Athabasca tar sands development along the Athabasca River. The entire Athabasca Basin, and especially the land south of the lake, is home to the world's richest uranium deposits, as well as some of the world's largest uranium mines. Mining exploration reached feverish levels a few years ago, but has since eased off somewhat in the aftermath of the Fukushima nuclear plant disaster in Japan, as many nations pause to reconsider the "benefits" of nuclear power. We can only hope that the land of the giant beaver will continue to weave its magic for years to come.

Cool Digs
Igloo Homestay on the Arctic Tundra

Building an igloo.

Quick, name the centre of Canada. No, it's not Toronto, Ottawa, or even Winnipeg. The closest community to the geographic centre of the country is Baker Lake, Nunavut, about 1,600 kilometres north of Winnipeg, and a bit south of the Arctic Circle. Walk down the streets of this town of fewer than 2,000, and chances are that most conversations you'll hear are in neither of Canada's official languages.

It's mid-April. At our home in Saskatoon, everyone is enjoying the warm spring weather. Well...almost everyone. With down-filled coats, boots, and other winter gear in hand, we're off to the airport, catching a series of flights to Baker Lake where winter is still in full swing. We've been invited to take part in a practice run for a new tourism venture, where visitors would experience life in a traditional Inuit winter camp, living in igloos on the Arctic tundra. We'll be the guinea pigs. How can we resist?

Next day, we're in a completely different world. Gliding across the endless expanse of treeless tundra, our sled barely makes a sound except for small thumps as its runners cross low solid snowdrifts. The dogs, spread out ahead in a fan hitch, run at a steady pace until suddenly they sniff something in the distance. It's the familiar scent of caribou somewhere in the hills. Instinctively, they veer to the left and pick up speed. With no reins to control the dogs, the driver Samson relies on voice commands to steer. "Whoosh-ka, whoosh-ka" he calls out in a loud whisper, and the dogs understand they are to turn right and remain on course.

We are part of a caravan of dog sleds and snowmobiles heading south from Baker Lake, a 50-kilometre journey to the frozen shores of Pitz Lake where we will spend nearly a week living in an igloo. After a three-hour trip bouncing across the snow and ice we arrive at our new home – a large three-room igloo. We have to crouch to walk through the two-metre-long entranceway that opens up to a spacious living area. Connected by archways just high enough to crawl through, are two bedrooms, each with snow platforms for beds. We prepare these by laying down a canvas tarp on the snow, followed by layers of muskox and caribou hides, and finally down-filled sleeping bags.

We need three more igloos to accommodate everybody, so work begins almost immediately. Paul Attutuvaa noses around the camp, probing the snow here and there with his long knife to find the right type of snow. A younger member of the group, David Akaswnee, acts as interpreter for the older Inuit who speak only

Inuktitut, and tries to explain what's happening. "The snow has to be fresh but not too fresh, somewhere between hard and soft." It's not easy to explain; it's just something you know from experience.

Attutuvaa and Jacob Ikinilik begin building the igloo from the inside, cutting the snow blocks from within a circle drawn in the snow. Each block is trimmed with the snow knife and slid against the adjoining one, the friction helping to keep them in place in their ascending spiral formation. Near the top, the spirals become tighter and blocks are placed at increasingly steeper angles. Then with only a small opening at the very top, about a foot across, Attutuvaa carefully trims a final block to close in the perfect dome. The result is an intricate engineering marvel, but the two experienced men make it look like the simplest of tasks.

As the igloo nears completion, the men's wives, Martha Ikinilik and Hattie Attutuvaa, use home-made wooden shovels to break up the packed snow around the igloo. Then they throw the snow on the dome to seal the cracks between the blocks. In less than three hours, the spacious igloo is complete and Ikinilik stands back to consider the result. It still needs something – a window. Grabbing a long-handled chisel, he walks to Pitz Lake and finds a spot where the wind has exposed some smooth clear ice. He chisels out an ice block about two feet square and a half foot thick, then cuts a hole in the igloo and fits the window snugly in place.

While our goal is to experience authentic igloo life, our hosts decide to make an addition to the camp to accommodate visitors – an outdoor privy. Built of snow blocks like everything else, it ends up looking like a tall narrow igloo. It is soon dubbed the "igloo-loo".

We've been fortunate to have travelled out and set up camp in reasonably good weather, but near evening it looks like our luck may be changing. Clouds gather on the horizon, glowing yellow-gold from the low sun, while the bluish-tinged, hard packed snow glistens as if coated with varnish. The wind picks up, sending drifting snow across the endless expanse. We have shelter but the dogs have to make do. They hunker down, some curling up into tight balls, noses tucked into tails, as drifts start to build around them.

Next morning we wake to a violent storm, forcing us to shovel our way out of the igloo entrance, now packed with snow. Before coming out, it is almost impossible to tell what is happening outside. The rounded aerodynamic shape of an igloo is the perfect building to withstand a blizzard. Other than snow in the entrance, it remains unscathed by the storm. Once outside, we're faced with a complete whiteout. The biting wind and snow, the ground, sky, even our igloo blend into a violent sea of white. Only steps away from the igloo, everything becomes invisible, with no way to tell which direction we're facing. The igloo-loo is only about 20 metres away, but we stick poles in the ground and string a rope to guide us when going between the two. We now have a much better understanding of how easy it would be to become lost or disoriented in that short distance, and how people can freeze to death just metres from safety.

The stormy weather lasts a couple of days, and we aren't able to go far or do much. One afternoon, Attutuvaa comes into our igloo, bringing chunks of caribou meat to make a stew. We first assumed that he had brought the meat from Baker Lake. But no, he had just come back from hunting. After all, the main purpose of an igloo camp is to hunt caribou, so Attutuvaa isn't going to let a minor inconvenience like a raging blizzard get in the way.

Few things are more important than caribou. Inuit throughout the Arctic have long depended on caribou, but for those who lived in inland regions, such as around here, caribou took on an added significance. Inuit living near the coast had access to seal and other sea creatures, but to those living inland, caribou was simply a matter of life or death. After providing a reasonably dependable source of food for years, something went terribly wrong in the 1950s when migrating caribou herds took a different route. Many Caribou Inuit faced starvation. This serious famine led the government to establish permanent settlements in places such as Baker Lake, moving many people off the land. For better or worse, this controversial move marked a profound change in the life of the Inuit, ending their semi-nomadic way of life, and making them dependent on settled communities. While hunting caribou continued to be important, many of the traditional ways began dying out, especially with younger generations who were born and brought up in town rather than out on the land.

Old timers such as Attutuvaa and Ikinilik are still well versed in the old ways, some of the last to personally experience a way of life that is fast disappearing. Spending a week with them proves to be nothing less than a rare glimpse into a bygone era.

Since the purpose of the trip is to relive the old ways, the Inuit dress in caribou clothing, rather than the modern snowmobile suits favoured today. The women go about their daily work inside the new igloo, sitting on the snow platform covered with caribou skins, a bluish light streaming through the ice window. They use traditional curved knives called ulus to prepare caribou hides for making boots and mitts. First they scrape the hides and trim the hair, then soften the hides by chewing and massaging them. To sew the pieces together, they use strands of caribou sinew for thread. A big piece of raw frozen caribou meat sits between the two women. Every once in a while, they use their razor-sharp ulus to shave off a thin slice of meat for a nice snack.

Today, everyone uses dark sunglasses as protection against snow blindness. In this land of white, white, and more white, the constant glare can become almost unbearable without protection. Jacob Ikinilik demonstrates an age-old solution to this problem. Taking a flat piece of wood, he fashions "glasses" that consist of very narrow slits, allowing only a thin sliver of light to hit the eyes. When wood wasn't available in this treeless landscape, they used carved caribou bone, and held the glasses in place with braided pieces of caribou sinew.

Outside, the men demonstrate how to apply mud on sled runners. First, they gather dirt from hillocks where the snow is shallow, mix it with warm water to form a sticky paste, then apply it evenly to the runners of the overturned sled. Everything is left to freeze overnight. The next day, they scrape the mud with a sharp knife to form a smooth surface. While nylon and steel runners are more commonly used now, some dog team owners still prefer mud, claiming that it performs better in the bitterly cold temperatures of mid-winter.

The three Inuit children in the camp play outside almost non-stop, regardless of the weather. Any doubts we have about igloos being durable quickly vanish as we watch these three scamper to the top and slide down the other side.

In these cold conditions, we gain a new respect for caribou products when wearing boots made from caribou hide. The biggest challenge in living in snow is keeping your feet warm. We bring good quality winter boots with us, but they're not nearly as warm as the caribou boots we are given to try. The term "boots" suggests substantial, heavy footwear, yet these are anything but. Although they come high above the ankles like traditional boots, they have the feel and weight of bedroom slippers. It's almost magical how something so seemingly flimsy can be so effective. This is footwear for dry cold snow only. The most important thing we have to remember is to brush the snow off our boots immediately after coming inside the igloo. If the snow melts on the caribou skin, our feet would soon get wet and cold.

While the inside of the igloo feels reasonably comfortable, the temperature is still below freezing. It has to be, considering what the dwelling is made of. Cooking inside can be tricky. We have to be careful not to turn our campstove higher than absolutely necessary. Heat causes an icy glaze on the interior walls, so that the snow no longer breathes. Besides, it's not a good idea to melt your house.

When the weather improves somewhat, it's time to go fishing. With lake ice still close to two metres thick, it takes a lot of effort with a long-handled chisel to break through, scoop out the icy debris, and make a small hole. Our fishing gear is basic – a hook on the end of a line tied to a curved piece of caribou antler fashioned into a handle. After jigging for a while, there's a sharp tug, and up comes a lake trout that barely fits through the hole. Ice starts to form in the hole very quickly, so if we don't keep it open it will freeze solid before long. With fresh lake trout and fresh caribou meat readily available, we rarely dip into the packaged store-bought food from town.

We settle into some of the day to day camp chores – catching fish, melting ice for drinking water, looking after the dogs, helping to build or repair igloos. We gain a tremendous admiration for people who not only have the skills to thrive in such a harsh and challenging environment, but appear completely at ease. It's obvious that the Ikiniliks and Attutuvaas really enjoy showing us how things were done in the old days. Through much of the trip, Jacob Ikinilik had been working on a soapstone carving, portraying a stylized man with his face looking up. He finishes the carving by the last day, and presents it to us as a parting gift.

When it's time to return to Baker Lake, we're treated to yet another whiteout, this time caused by ice fog. We head off into the eerie monochrome landscape with no horizon, as people and dog teams seem to float in a sea of nothingness. Landmarks are invisible and our tracks have long since been obliterated by the storm. Ikinilik and Attutuvaa lead the way into the white void. No compass or GPS for these guys – they navigate by the feel of the wind and the angle of the snowdrifts. After a couple hours, we stop for a rest and bring out the thermoses of hot tea to help warm up. Ikinilik and Attutuvaa have a serious-looking discussion in Inuktitut, gesturing in different directions as if they're discussing the route home. Back onto the sleds, we float and bounce through the endless void for a couple more hours. Then as we come over a slight ridge, faint grey shapes loom far in the distance, and the buildings of Baker Lake begin to stand out. We're right on course.

The last reality check for us comes on the flight home. When travelling to most exotic places in the world, a final step on the homeward journey is going through the rigmarole of passport and customs checks. This time, however, it's simply a matter of getting off the plane – no customs, no passports, nothing. While it ranks among the most exotic trips we've ever taken, we're not returning from some far-flung corner of the globe, but from the centre of Canada.

Going with the Floe
Harp Seals in the Gulf of St. Lawrence

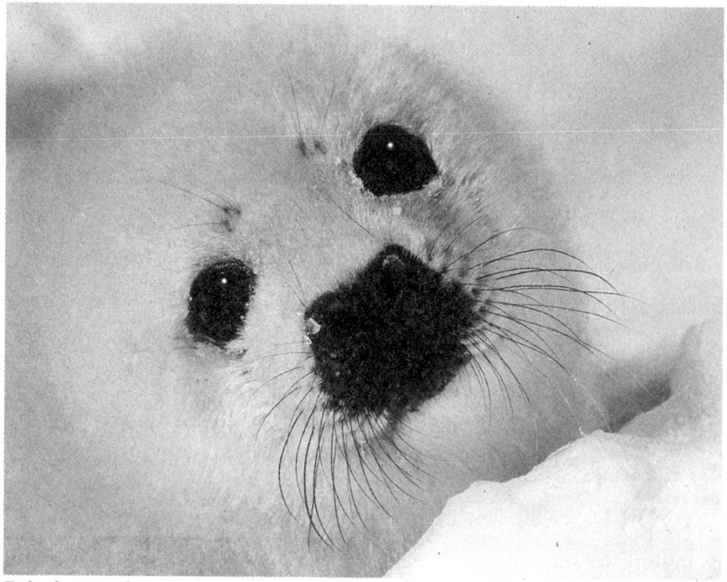

Baby harp seal.

Clouds of snow swirl around us like a blizzard as the five helicopters rev up their engines. We lift off into the clear sky, rising above the Château Madelinot, then soaring over the spectacular red cliffs of Quebec's Magdalen Islands and a sand dune-laden spit before heading out to sea. We soon lose sight of land altogether as our fleet of brilliant red, white, and blue Canadian Helicopters flies in formation just 50 metres above the icy Gulf of St. Lawrence. Below us, we see nothing but water and ice, the floes artistically arranged in an abstract seascape of white and blue.

Top: *Sunset over the Simien Mountains.*

Middle: *Arlene Karpan with scout Jemale (left), and guide Getachew (right).*

Right: *Gelada baboons.*

Top: *Rhino crossing the road in Kruger National Park.*

Middle: *A car is dwarfed by a bull elephant in Addo Elephant National Park.*

Below: *Mating lions in Kruger National Park.*

Top: *Ostrich in the Kalahari Desert. This normally dry terrain comes alive after a heavy rain.*
Middle: *Cheetah on the prowl.*
Below: *Wildebeest at sunrise in the Kalahari.*

Top: *Gemsbok in the Namib Desert.*

Middle: *A young springbok pronking.*

Below: *Leopard relaxing in a camelthorn tree.*

Top: *Dunes at Sossusvlei in the Namib Desert.*

Middle: *Desiccated trees at Dead Vlei in the Namib Desert.*

Left: *Quiver Tree Forest in southern Namibia.*

The dunes in Namibia (top) are in dry desert with no water around, while the dunes of Athabasca are sliced by rivers such as the William.

Right: *Sand at varying depths forms the riverbed of the William.*

Top: *The William River seen from the air. The varying depths of sand on the riverbed give the look of butterscotch pudding marbled with whipped cream.*

Below: *The exhumed forest of Thomson Bay is bathed in a red glow as the sun sets over Lake Athabasca.*

Top: *Repairing a sled.*

Middle: *Building an igloo.*

Below: *Life inside the igloo.*

Visiting harp seals on an ice floe in the Gulf of St. Lawrence.

Top: *Moai at Tongariki.*

Below: *Moai at the base of the quarry at Rano Raraku.*

Top: *Rano Kau crater.*

Middle: *Moai with red topknots at Anakena Beach.*

Below: *The rugged volcanic shoreline of Easter Island.*

***Top:** The Copper Canyon railway makes two 180-degree turns including one entirely inside a tunnel near Temoris.*

***Middle:** Train approaching Divisadero station.*

***Below:** The cliffs of the Copper Canyon near Divisadero.*

Monarch butterflies take flight at their overwintering site near Angangueo, Mexico.

Top: *The rising sun illuminates the spires of Mount Fitzroy in Argentina.*

Below: *Torres del Paine National Park, Chile.*

Top: *Perito Moreno Glacier, Argentina.*

Middle: *Guanacos.*

Below: *Monte León National Park along the Atlantic coast of Argentina.*

Top: P/V Mariya Yermolova *in Neko Harbour, Antarctica.*

Middle: *Storm clouds near the Lemaire Channel.*

Below: *Gentoo penguin and chick.*

Forty minutes after takeoff, we swoop over a mass of pack ice a half kilometre across, hosting hundreds of harp seals – right now mere black and grey specks against a pure white world. No matter how much we read about the intricate life cycle of the harp seal, finding them in the "middle of nowhere" still comes as a surprise. Of course, to mother seals, this isn't nowhere at all, but a very special place they have travelled thousands of kilometres to reach and give birth – the perfect nursery. We're feeling fortunate that this is a cold winter. For harp seals and seal watchers alike, cold is good; it means that more sea ice forms and the seals will be reasonably close by.

It's not until the helicopters circle a couple times and come in lower that we glimpse what visitors from around the world come to see – resplendent white, newborn seal pups perfectly camouflaged among the chunks of snow and ice, their soft fur and black saucer-like eyes now an international symbol for cuteness. Along with a couple dozen other visitors, we are on this guided excursion specifically to get up close and personal with the white-coats.

We're not the only visitors, though. The seals are transients too. Summering in waters near the eastern Arctic islands, harps are among the more abundant seals in the world, with the population in Canadian waters alone estimated at more than five million, up from about two million in the 1970s. Come September, these sea mammals begin migrating southward, with one large herd staying near Newfoundland and the other swimming into the Gulf of St. Lawrence near the Magdalen Islands, a half-moon-shaped archipelago of a dozen islands, about 100 kilometres north of Prince Edward Island. Here, on the great ice pack off the islands, they give birth around the end of February and early March.

Outside the helicopter on the pack ice, we strap crampons on our boots to minimize slipping, and grip ski poles for stability.

Outfitted in identical brilliant orange or yellow survival suits to keep us warm in sub-zero temperatures, we carefully pick our way across this exotic frozen world in the middle of the sea. We're the awkward ones; the seals, on the other hand, simply slide across the surface with ease.

As we walk among the mothers and babies, we spy some pups nursing, though most have been left on their own while their moms are away feeding. Most pups are quiet, but across the ice floe we hear the constant, plaintive high-pitched cries of "maaaa…maaaa" that sounds part human and part bleating lamb. Now and then a mother seal pops her head up through an air hole in the ice, takes a quick look around, then dives back in. While photographing one baby seal, we are startled as its mother suddenly comes shooting up from an air hole and thumps across the ice behind us with frightening speed. She goes straight to her baby without bothering us, but it becomes apparent that getting close to a mother is not a good idea.

This mothering instinct is fleeting among harp seals, and the pups are expected to grow up quickly. Their distinctive white coats last less than two weeks. During this time, they nurse on milk that is 10 times richer than that of cows. About 12-14 days after giving birth to 10-kilogram pups, the mothers abandon these seemingly helpless balls of fluff, and swim off to mate with waiting males on nearby floes. The pups don't eat for the next month or so, living off their reserves of blubber. Eventually, they learn to dive for fish, and when fully mature, will weigh over 100 kilograms. In spring and early summer, the seal herds head north as the sea ice gradually melts. When they reach the Arctic waters near Baffin Island, they will have completed a round trip of over 3,000 kilometres. At the end of the short Arctic summer, they are ready to turn around and do it all again.

The highlight is getting right up to the pups. The occasional one hisses or turns away, but for the most part they are either inquisitive or completely ignore us. One rolls over like a dog. A couple pups play by repeatedly dragging themselves up a sloping block of ice then sliding down. One pup resembles a plump, pure white roll of fuzz with black eyes, nose, and a few whiskers stuck on one end. It appears completely relaxed as it looks up at us with those enormous eyes, and allows us to reach out to touch its unbelievably soft fur.

Back at the hotel, we celebrate our first day out and look forward to returning to the ice floes the following morning. But the weather has other plans. We wake to howling winds and a heavy snow storm. The helicopters are grounded, so we won't be able to return to the ice until at least the following day. This is why tour operators highly recommend building one or two "weather days" into itineraries. It's not a lost day at all, but a chance to explore more of the islands.

The Magdalen Islands are an archipelago of 12 islands, six of which are connected by roads along thin spits of land consisting of mostly sand dunes. Part of the province of Quebec, the islands are closer to Prince Edward Island and Cape Breton Island than to mainland Quebec. This isolation for many years has developed a distinct culture which is part Québécois and part Acadian, the French-speaking culture of the Maritime provinces.

The land is incredibly varied for a small area, with sloping hilly plains ending in spectacular red cliffs, forested interiors, some 300 kilometres of beaches, and sand dunes practically everywhere. Sparsely populated, there's only 13,000 residents spread throughout the islands, many living in wooden houses painted brilliant colours. The economy depends on fishing, with mussels standing out as one specialty. Tourism is becoming increasingly important, with two major seasons – summer because of the legendary beaches and other natural attractions such as nature preserves, birding, and sea kayaking, as well as a short winter tourist season centred around the seals.

Another winter diversion is dog sledding. We decide to join the dozen or so other visitors for an afternoon excursion. We sip coffee around the wood-burning stove in the warm-up shelter while the crew busily hitches up the sleds. Anxious dogs jump, howl, and bark in a chaotic jumble of noise. But once we're seated in our sleds and the dogs are released, the noise almost magically ceases. The only sound is sled runners scraping through ice and snow, and mushers occasionally shouting commands to the dogs.

Our first impression of the Magdalen Islands was a land dominated by open windswept beaches, but it's completely different here in the interior of Ile du Cap-aux-Meules, the main island. We're racing along a narrow trail that twists and turns over hummocky hills covered in thick forest, as trees fly by just inches away.

Eventually we emerge from the forest and speed along the clifftops of the rugged shore, the vertical slopes looking like dripping white icing on a cake, formed from repeated freezing and thawing of the thick ice and snow. The highlight comes near the end of the trip when we stop along the shore and the guides lead us to the cliff edge where one gentle slope is draped in perfectly smooth ice – the ultimate frozen water slide! We sit on the top in our nylon survival suits then slide down, yelling like a bunch of six-year-olds, landing in the soft snow at the bottom. A short walk along the frozen sea shore brings us to a narrow cave where we crawl inside to discover an enchanted cathedral-like world with blue-tinged icicles suspended from the roof.

The Seal Interpretation Centre has everything you could ever hope to know about seals – their biology, migration, how they fit into the food chain, and their importance to these islands. Seal hunting has always been an integral part of the local culture and economy. Our hotel restaurant even offers seal meat on the menu. But seal hunting remains controversial. The centre doesn't shy away from the controversy, but rather presents both sides of the story, with the stated objective of encouraging visitors to decide for themselves. Organizations objecting to the hunt usually use images of cute, white baby harp seals, although it's been illegal to hunt white-coats for many years. As in most controversial issues, the reality is usually more complex than what we see in short news clips.

Next morning is crisp and cold but clear, so we're able to return to the ice floes. Our second visit is every bit as rewarding as the first, and now we're slightly more adept at making our way around the slippery surface. We can't help thinking that when it comes to getting close to wildlife, this ranks right up there with great wildlife excursions anywhere in the world – but with one big difference. On most trips the rule is "look but don't touch." Here we can not only approach the baby white-coats, but also touch or pet them. Biologists indicate that petting the baby seals does them no harm. Visitors are few, guides oversee things, and the season is very short.

We're surprised that so many visitors are from Japan. Later we meet a tour operator who arranges trips for Japanese and ask her what it is about seals that attracts them, because we don't see as many Japanese on other wildlife trips. She answers without hesitation, "Because they can touch them."

The Moai the Merrier
Unravelling the Mysteries of Easter Island

Moai at Rano Raraku quarry.

The captain comes on the speaker and announces that we'll be landing in a few minutes. Looking out the window, we can't help but wonder, "Land where?" It's been close to five hours since our flight left Santiago and for the entire time there's been nothing but ocean, ocean, and more ocean. But undoubtedly the pilot has found the small spec of land in the middle of the Pacific, far away from...everywhere.

Easter Island is considered the most remote permanently inhabited place on Earth. It's 3,600 kilometres west of the Chilean mainland, on the way to nowhere. If we were to continue travelling west, the next sizable piece of land with regular air service is Tahiti, another five hours' flying time. The nearest inhabited island is tiny Pitcairn Island, with around 50 people, over 2,000 kilometres away. Yet isolated Easter Island holds some of the world's most dramatic and mysterious sights, with a beguiling past and riddles not yet solved.

We land at the airport, having made no arrangements. Some guest house operators have desks at the arrivals area just for visitors like us. As we glance at their offerings, one woman obviously anxious for business waves us over and assures us that she undoubtedly has the best place and the best deal. Since we're staying longer than the average visitor, she offers us a special rate. It turns out to be a good choice, a pleasant house set among tropical flowers and fruit trees, where Theresa and her mother Maria live, and offer extra rooms to guests.

Under 4,000 people live on the island, almost all of them in the only town, Hanga Roa. Businesses stretch along a few main streets – a couple basic supermarkets, a handful of restaurants, tour offices where you can rent cars or bicycles, a fruit and vegetable market, and of course the inevitable souvenir stands. Most accommodation offerings are guest houses, such as where we're staying, or small hotels. Thankfully, there are no high-rise hotels dominating the skyline or sprawling resorts as in many island destinations.

One modern facility, however, is done on a grand scale – the airport runway. At 3,300 metres or over 10,000 feet long, it looks oversized for such a small island. It was expanded a number of years ago with the help of NASA, making it an emergency landing strip for space shuttles in case they run into trouble over the vast Pacific.

The volcanic island supports only limited agriculture. Fruit grows in abundance, but most supplies come from the mainland. Our first day there, we head to the supermarket to buy a rotisserie roasted chicken to take home for supper. A couple days later, we go back for another.

"Sorry, all out of chicken," says the cashier.

"When will you be getting more?" we ask.

"No idea," she replies, "Whenever they get here. Could be next week; maybe longer."

It seems that not all of the inscrutable things about Easter Island are from the past. The islanders have a long history with chickens, thought to be the only domestic livestock brought by the original Polynesian settlers several hundred years ago. Crowing roosters and a chorus of raucous chickens wake us before dawn every morning, and the cackling birds wander freely practically everywhere we go. Yet the supermarket has to wait until they're shipped from the mainland.

Scholars vary in their estimates of when people first inhabited the island, anytime from the first few centuries AD, to closer to 900 AD. The most easterly outpost of Polynesia, the island is known locally as Rapa Nui. The Easter Island name originated when Dutch explorer Jacob Roggeveen happened by on Easter Day, 1722, making the first recorded contact between the island and the outside world. During those many years of isolation, the island experienced amazing achievements, the most famous of which are the numerous moai dotting the island. These gigantic stone statues with their long angular heads are thought to represent high ranking ancestors. Most were built and transported between 1000 and 1600 AD, without the use of machines, draft animals, or even metal tools.

Somewhere along the way, society began to break down. Internal wars erupted, and part of this involved toppling over your enemy's moai. When Captain Cook stopped here in 1774, he noted that several statues had been toppled. By the mid-1800s, reports from visiting ships indicated no standing statues at all. Not only did islanders suffer internal strife, but contact with the outside world brought smallpox and other diseases. Things went from bad to worse when Peruvian slave traders captured some 1,500 islanders in the 1860s, taking them to work in mines. In 1877, the island's population hit a low of only 111.

Chile annexed Easter Island in 1888, and it essentially became a giant sheep ranch. It wasn't until 1966 that the islanders became Chilean citizens and the fortunes of this Pacific spec began to turn around. Today, the island has one foot in Polynesia and the other in South America. Roughly half of the 4,000 or so people are ethnically Rapa Nui, while the other half come from the mainland. The working language is Spanish, although the local Polynesian language, also called Rapa Nui, is widely spoken as well. When we listen to Theresa talking to her friends or family, she speaks in Rapa Nui, with a generous sprinkling of Spanish words. Rapa Nui is also spoken at services at the church of Santa Cruz where traditional Polynesian beliefs and motifs meld with Catholicism.

We don't have to go far to see our first moai. The Tahai site is a short walk from the edge of town where three ahu or ceremonial platforms stand next to the sea. Thought to have been an important sacred centre, the site was restored in the 1970s. One ahu has five moai in various styles and states of preservation. The second platform has a single statue considered to be among the oldest on the island. The third, named Ahu Ko te Riku, is one of the most impressive and widely photographed moai, its head crowned with a heavy red topknot. Unique to the island, it has eyes of white coral and jet-black obsidian, making it come alive as it stands near the shoreline, staring back at us. It is believed that many moai once had eyes, but they all "lost their sight" over time. Tahai becomes our favourite place for sunset most evenings, watching the sun dip into the Pacific, framed by massive heads that become imposing silhouettes against the glow of twilight.

Anxious to see more, we arrange for Theresa's brother-in-law, Patricio, to take us around the island, which only has a couple major roads. Covering around 170 square kilometres, the island is shaped like a triangle, with volcano craters marking each corner. A striking first impression is the wildness of the shoreline, with towering sea cliffs and chaotic jumbles of boulders. The basalt rock resembles fresh lava flow with ragged and sharp edges, much of it as black as coal. Unlike most Polynesian islands, Easter Island has no coral reefs, so the sea pounds it relentlessly on all sides.

Our first stop is Ahu Vinapu, a stone's throw from the airport runway. We see remains of toppled moai, but most remarkable is the ahu or ceremonial platform where statues once stood. Largely unrestored, the wall is built of enormous boulders, fitted together with such intricate precision that we would be hard pressed to stick a pin in the cracks. Gazing at the fine workmanship, we're reminded of the ancient Inca walls of Peru, in places like Cusco. It was remarkable similarities like this that led Norwegian ethnographer and explorer, Thor Heyerdahl, to speculate that the island had been colonized from, or greatly influenced by, ancient South America.

Heyerdahl's famous Kon Tiki expedition in 1947 showed that it was possible to sail a primitive reed raft from South America to islands in the South Pacific. He later led a major archaeological expedition to Easter Island in 1955–56, followed by his bestselling book, *Aku-Aku*, that asserts the South American origins theory. Subsequent research, however, hasn't supported Heyerdahl; the accepted view today is that early Easter Island settlement came solely from Polynesia.

We're expecting to see a lot of moai. After all, it was seeing photographs of those intriguing heads and reading the fascinating legends that brought us to this remote corner of the world. But what we're not prepared for is the overwhelming scale of it all. Travelling around the island, we pass one site after another, some with standing moai, but mostly toppled statues lying prostrate, abandoned and ignored after ancient battles. Add to these the remains of walls, altars, caves, foundations, and rock carvings, and we're faced with a staggering display of antiquity.

Nothing we read before visiting prepared us for climbing up the volcano of Rano Raraku, the birthplace of the moai. Slopes of the ancient quarry are covered in standing, toppled, and unfinished statues. Mostly upright heads lie scattered at the base of the volcano. While it may look like these are simply heads, excavations revealed that they do indeed have bodies. Erosion and accumulating soil deposits over hundreds of years have buried some statues up to their necks and noses. Researchers excavating one of the larger statues found that two-thirds of it was underground. Is it thought that these finished moai were awaiting transport to other parts of the islands.

As we walk farther up the slopes that reach about 100 metres or so above the sea, we're astonished to see moai literally everywhere we look, right up to the crest of the volcano. Climbing over the ridge, we descend the slopes toward the volcanic lake. And what do we find? More moai. Lots of them.

Most statues are unfinished, some in the early stages of carving, while others are so complete that only final touches would be needed to free them from their stony birthplace. Carvers using stone tools first removed the volcanic rock to create a niche or hollowed-out cavity for their work area. Then they set about carving the moai, and refining its features. When complete, more rock was removed to release the statue. It was set upright so work on the back could be finished. At last it was ready to be moved to its final location. Only about a third of them ever made it.

Around 900 moai have been counted on the island, close to half of them right here. It's the number of unfinished statues, suspended in the midst of creation, that we find most mind-boggling. They didn't simply build one, put it up, then go on to the next one. Huge numbers were being carved at the same time. What an incredible sight this would have been. Then all of a sudden, they stopped, so abruptly that it looks like carvers simply dropped their tools on the spot. Perhaps the boss came by and said, "We've decided not to build statues anymore." Or perhaps workers, tired of the incessant toil, rebelled and said, "Take this job and shove it!" Or were there other reasons? Like practically everything to do with Easter Island's past, conflicting theories abound.

Most moai range in size from two metres to over nine metres tall. The largest ever built was never finished and still lies in the quarry. Stretching over 20 metres or 65 feet long, it's estimated to weigh around 270 tons. If it were lifted, it would reach about the height of a five-story building. Speculation is that it was never finished because the carvers knew they had bitten off more than they could chew, and work was halted because they couldn't figure out how to move something that big.

So how did the gigantic statues get from the quarry to various sites around the island? At the crest of the Rano Raraku volcano we find a series of shallow round holes, about a metre across and more than a metre deep. Speculation is that the moai were lowered down the slope using ropes attached to thick support poles anchored in these holes. As for travelling several kilometres around the island, local legend says that the moai walked by themselves. Researchers have come up with various theories, one of which does involve "walking", where the upright statues would have been rocked from side to side using a fulcrum and ropes, as they slowly progressed along roadways. Other theories suggest that they were laid down and pulled along log rollers, or left standing and pulled on a sledge. There's no shortage of theories and research is still going on.

Travelling around the island, we see other tourists at the main sites, although nowhere does it feel crowded or overrun. When we rent a car, we're able to visit many off-the-beaten-track sites, and often there's no one else around. A highlight is returning to the Rano Raraku quarry late one day, just before sunset. We are the only ones here, as the low sun floods the gigantic grey heads with a warm radiance. It's as if the stone-faced titans are about to spring to life, and we have them all to ourselves.

From the ridge of the volcano, we look over the most spectacular finished moai site of them all, Tongariki, just over a kilometre away. A 200-metre-long platform holds 15 statues of various sizes and styles, their backs to the sea, and facing the quarry of Rano Raraku. The setting is stunning, with a bay of pounding surf, framed by high vertical cliffs rising straight from the sea. Like all other standing moai, these too were toppled during internal conflicts. To add insult to injury, a powerful tsunami hit the island in 1960, packing enough force to wash these sleeping behemoths up to 500 metres inland. A major restoration project started in 1992. Even with the help of a state-of-the-art crane brought in from Japan, it took almost four years to reconstruct the ahu and install the moai once more on the ceremonial platform. We can only imagine how long it took the original builders using stone tools, poles, and rope.

One morning, we get up before dawn to drive across the

island to be at Tongariki for sunrise. We meet no other traffic on the lonely road, but have to take it slow since horses are everywhere, grazing beside the road, often crossing, or just standing in the middle for no apparent reason. These aren't wild horses; each one belongs to somebody, yet they're left to wander anywhere and everywhere unattended. We arrive just as the sun starts to peek over the Pacific horizon, directly behind the statues. Mist rises from the pounding surf, and the low sun shining through casts a golden tinge. The silhouettes of the 15 monoliths throw long ghostly shadows that seem to stretch forever.

With the exception of another small piece of sandy shore nearby, Anakena Beach is the only beach on the island. It was here, according to legend, that the Polynesian chief Hotu Matu'a landed sometime in the distant past and founded Rapa Nui. This idyllic spot best fits preconceived ideas of what a Polynesian island should look like, with a grove of coconut palms overlooking a brilliantly white sand beach, backed by the sparkling turquoise Pacific. We spend a day here, swimming in the inviting water and relaxing on the sand.

But this is beach life Easter Island style. Along with sand, sea, and palm trees, megalithic monsters are also looking over us. One ahu has seven moai, four of which sport huge red topknots. These are considered among the best preserved statues on the island because, when toppled, they landed in soft sand rather than on rocks like almost everywhere else. The other ahu has a single moai. During Thor Heyerdahl's 1956 expedition, this became the first statue in modern times to be reinstalled in its original position. It took 12 men 18 days to raise the 20-ton monster. They used nothing but poles and stones, slowing prying up the statue while jamming in more and more stones to support it.

A short drive away along the north coast, we come to the biggest moai ever moved from the quarry site – 11 metres tall and weighing around 80 tons. Known as Paro, it looks rather forlorn lying face down. It is thought that Paro was the last moai to be toppled, possibly around 1840. This site is equally famous for a smooth round rock about half a metre across which, according to legend, was brought by Hotu Matu'a. Said to represent the "navel of the world", this strange rock seems to give off some kind of energy, so when we place our hands on it, then pull them away, there's a slight tingling sensation. We hold a compass near the rock and it goes berserk, pointing different directions depending upon how close it is to the rock.

The standard procedure for erecting moai was to put them near the shore but facing inland. One suggested reason for this is that the statues would then watch over the villages. Driving down a minor interior road, we come to Ahu Akivi, the only exception to this practice, where seven moai stand atop an ahu about two kilometres from the coast and, unlike everywhere else, they face the ocean. One legend says that these represent early settlers from other parts of Polynesia who are looking out toward their former home.

A bit farther along that minor interior road we come to Puna Pau, a smaller crater with red volcanic rock. This is the quarry for the pukao, the round red headdress or topknot placed on the heads of some moai. About 20 remain in various states of completion, including some that are finished and adorned with carvings. Moving these stones, which are up to two metres high, would have been a tremendous job, as would placing them on top of the moai. Similar to the quarry for moai, work here seems to have stopped suddenly.

Everywhere we go, we're struck by the windswept, wide open nature of the island. It must have looked like this for hundreds of years, since Roggeveen mentioned the lack of trees in 1722. Yet scientific studies show that the island was once covered in thick forest, including tall trees such as the giant palm. Trees were used for firewood, building canoes, to make rope and poles to help move the moai, and were cleared for gardens. While researchers do not all agree on exactly how the statues were moved, any method would have involved ropes and at least some wooden poles. So once the source for these materials had been depleted, it would no longer have been possible to keep moving moai. One theory is that work on moai stopped simply because they ran out of materials to move them.

Today the island does have some trees, mostly fast-growing non-native eucalyptus. Native species are also being grown in the hopes that one day they will repopulate the landscape.

To see some of Easter Island's post-moai history, we head in the opposite direction from Hanga Roa, to the western tip of the island. We walk along the shore past the naval base, where a couple daring surfers ride the mighty waves. A protected bay is filled with fishing boats, watched over by yet another moai. One boat heads to sea, and is buffeted by strong waves almost immediately after leaving shore. Somehow the boat operator guides his bouncing craft along a safe route through waves and past dangerous rocks. Beyond, the shoreline becomes even wilder. The land rises sharply into high cliffs of exposed black rocks that look as if freshly flowing lava has just solidified. Yet, the rock is no match for the relentless pounding waves that have worn countless contours and caves into the sea cliffs.

We're searching for the island's most famous cave, Ana Kai Tangata, the so-called "Cannibal Cave", said to be site of cannibal feasts. Since its opening faces directly into the surf, we can only enter when it isn't too rough, and even then we have to carefully make our way over wet rocks. Looking up at the cave ceiling, we see that it is covered with paintings of red birds outlined in white. The dark conditions have preserved the old but still vibrant pictographs. Ancient rock art abounds on the island, with paintings such as these, and even more numerous petroglyphs, images etched into stone.

An astounding 4,000 or so rock art images have been discovered throughout this small island, but none so spectacular as those at Orongo ceremonial village, at the end of our walk to the island's western tip. It's the magnificent location that sets this place apart, perched high on a narrow ridge between Rano Kau volcano and the sea. One side of Orongo looks over the crater of the extinct volcano that spans well over a kilometre across, with steep and treacherous 200-metre walls dropping to a crater lake that legend says is bottomless. The other is right on the edge of a 300-metre vertical precipice rising straight out of the sea. We walk along this razor edge past two rows of low oval-shaped stone houses that were central to this sacred site. Just beyond, elaborate petroglyphs cover the rocky outcroppings; motifs of birds, sea creatures, turtles, human faces, and designs whose meanings are lost in time have been painstakingly etched into the surface of the stone. Most notable are carvings of the Bird Man, a crouching man with a bird's head.

After the moai craze ran its course, Easter Islanders adopted an even stranger obsession – the Bird Man cult. Each year the major clans would appoint representatives to take part in a remarkable race. From this spot, competitors descended the 300-metre cliff to the inhospitable shoreline, then using bundles of floating reeds, swam two kilometres through strong current and shark-infested water to the tiny islet of Motu Mui. Their task was to find the first egg laid by a sooty tern that season, then swim back trying not to break the fragile cargo. The first competitor to successfully complete this mission would present the egg to his master, who would then hold the prestigious position of Bird Man, the island's head honcho, for the next year.

The Bird Man lived away from other people, where he would not bathe, and let his hair and fingernails grow. One of the perks of the job is that the Bird Man could decide who should be sacrificed in order to assure prosperity for the coming year. A handy way to get rid of people you don't like, but his decisions often led to controversy and renewed conflicts and battles. According to reports by missionaries, Bird Man rituals endured until the late 1800s.

The island's outstanding accomplishments were followed by a downward spiral, then eventual collapse. A widely held, though certainly not universal, view is that Easter Island destroyed its civilization by overexploiting its resources. Deforestation would have meant no more firewood, no more canoes for fishing, erosion, loss of soil fertility, and a host of other repercussions. The world has seen a lot of civilizations collapse over the years, but in most places, people move away to start over, or rebuild as other civilizations take over. But in this remote corner of the world, there was nowhere to go and no one to take over. The demise of Easter Island is often used as a metaphor for the impending collapse of Earth, that the same fate awaits us if we aren't careful.

Of course, nothing is ever simple on Easter Island. The more we travel around this island and look into its past, the more it becomes apparent that unravelling its secrets is a work in progress. A long list of experts over the years claim to have solved the mysteries of Easter Island, only to have other equally credible experts come up with different interpretations. Were the islanders masters of their own destruction through mismanagement, or did they suffer some ecological catastrophe beyond their control, such as climate change? Or should we look more to their disastrous contacts with the outside world? It depends on whom you ask.

Such puzzles make Easter Island all the more compelling. Along with wondrous landscapes and astonishing ancient monuments, part of the enduring enchantment of travelling here is that it remains an island of mystery. The stone-faced statues don't give up their secrets easily.

CHIHUAHUA CHOO CHOO
Back on the Rails in the Copper Canyon

Train conductor at Divisadero station.

One breathtaking scene after another flashes by as we cling to mountain sides overlooking deep green valleys, plunge through tunnel after tunnel, and cross a series of bridges spanning rivers and rugged gorges. We're on one of the world's great train journeys, travelling through Mexico's most striking wilderness landscape.

Considered an engineering marvel when it was completed in 1961, the Chihuahua al Pacifico Railroad, or "El Chepe", runs for 650 kilometres. From near sea level at Los Mochis, it crosses coastal plains and rich farmland, weaves through foothills and semi-tropical forest, then climbs to over 2,400 metres through the Sierra Madre Occidental Mountains, skirting one of the largest and deepest canyons anywhere, before ending in the high plains near the Chihuahua desert. Along the way, we cross 37 bridges, the longest almost a half kilometre long, the highest over 100 metres. We go through 86 tunnels, the longest over 1.5 kilometres, and another that makes a 180-degree turn completely inside a mountain.

Each day two trains – a first class train, and a second or "economic" class – run each way between Los Mochis near the Pacific coast, and the city of Chihuahua. As a general rule, package tourists usually opt for the first class train, while locals who live along the route, school groups, and independent travellers often take the second class one. There isn't a significant difference; first class has newer cars, along with a dining and bar car, and takes less time to complete the journey.

This is a return trip for us. The first time we travelled first class, but this time we decide to try the economic class after someone points out that it might be better for photography since this train goes slower and makes more stops. The fact that second class is exactly half the price of first class comes as an added bonus. On our first trip, we started at Los Mochis, travelled through the most impressive sections of the route to Divisadero, then back again. This time, we start from the Chihuahua side, and take our time by breaking the journey along the way. What we're looking forward to most is travelling down into the yawning canyon.

Chihuahua is the capital city of the State of Chihuahua, the largest state by area in the country. Even in the midst of the city, there's no mistaking that we're in cowboy country. On one street in the market area, we pass a series of shops selling nothing but cowboy boots – elaborate, high-heeled, pointy-toed extravaganzas in every colour and style you can imagine. The nearby centre square pays tribute to the city's name-sake, the Chihuahua dog, with several colourful and whimsical statues of the tiny, big-eared mutt. Above all, Chihuahua is famous as the home of Pancho Villa, the controversial bandit turned military general, and revolutionary folk hero. Villa's house is home to a museum with everything to do with his life and the 1910 revolution, including posters urging recruits to "Ride with Pancho Villa for Gold and Glory!", and the bullet-ridden car from his 1923 assassination.

Heading west from Chihuahua, it's around 200 kilometres before we reach the canyon lands. We pass through semi-arid plains, then the flourishing farmlands and orchards around Cuauhtémoc, home to most of Mexico's German-speaking Mennonites, descendants of those who emigrated from the Canadian prairies in the 1920s.

The most popular stop along the railway, and informal "gateway to the canyons" is Creel, a town of around 10,000 people, 250 kilometres west of Chihuahua. We happen to arrive during the town's 100th anniversary celebration, which makes this practically a new town by Mexican standards. Creel owes its existence to the timber industry, although in recent years, tourism has become increasingly important to the local economy.

Creel is the largest of the canyon towns and a prime jumping-off point for trips all around the canyon lands. We start with a day trip into the nearby hills, where in a relatively small area we find magnificent waterfalls, the Valley of the Mushrooms where strange rock formations resemble giant toadstools, the Valley of the Frogs with its squat amphibian-like boulders, along with historic mission churches. People living in these hills are primarily Tarahumara who cling to a traditional lifestyle, so traditional that some still live in caves fashioned into basic dwellings.

Tarahumara Indians, or Rarámuri as they are also known, are considered among the most traditional of Mexico's indigenous peoples. Living in these semi-isolated and thinly populated mountains, they have been able to preserve many customs. Women wearing brightly coloured clothes often set up stalls along tourist routes to sell traditional crafts, such as elaborate baskets woven from the long needles of Apache pines. The Tarahumara have a reputation as long distance runners, excelling in competitions such as ultra-marathons. We stop at one Tarahumara cave dwelling, a gaping hole in the side of a cliff. The ceiling has been blackened by years of smoke from open fires (it can get very cold). Cindercrete bricks serve as partial room dividers, and shelves made from old railway ties hold their belongings. Like most cultures trying to continue a traditional way of life, the Tarahumara have had to cope with increasing influences from the outside world. Some reports suggest that their biggest threat today comes from disruptions caused by Mexico's ongoing drug war.

Impressive as it is, the landscape near the canyon rim around Creel is just a teaser for what awaits. The town of Batopilas lies on the canyon floor, not far away, but there's over 1,800 metres, or well over a mile altitude difference, most of it almost straight down. A bus dubbed the "Dramamine Express" by travellers makes the run, but we end up making special arrangements with our guesthouse in Creel – the Casa Margaritas. Four other people staying here, a doctor and his wife from Tijuana, and a retired couple from France, are also looking for ways to make the trip. So the wheeler-dealer manager at Casa Margaritas soon comes up with a plan. They have a sister hotel in Batopilas, so he arranges for their van and driver to take us there, show us the sights, then bring us back two days later. It proves to be an ideal arrangement. With our own driver, we can make stops along the way on one of the most dramatic road trips anywhere.

It's only about a five-hour trip, but a world away. Our driver, Salvador, greets us decked out in a wide-brimmed cowboy hat, a fancy pair of blazing red cowboy boots just like those we saw in Chihuahua, accented with matching red belt. We start off along a smooth paved highway, but soon turn off onto a rough gravel road that is more like a winding rock pile. Most of the way, the dusty road clings to the side of the mountain and is little more than a lane wide. Forget about guard rails! We bounce along a series of dizzying hairpin turns with precipitous drops where the canyon walls appear to fall away almost beneath us. Fortunately, traffic is very light. At La Bufa lookout, we stop to look down the valley at a series of switchbacks extending a kilometre almost straight down. While it feels as if we're in the middle of remote wilderness, we still see the odd isolated house perched on mountain edges – the ultimate in living away from it all.

With such a steep descent, landscapes change quickly and markedly, from pine forests along the canyon rim, to transitional forest and craggy mountain slopes, then eventually onto the desert-like canyon floor dotted with cactus and agave. Before leaving Creel that cool November morning, the heater was on in our hotel room. Later the same day in Batopilas, the ceiling fan whirs away full tilt to provide relief from the sub-tropical heat.

Long and narrow Batopilas lies sandwiched between the Batopilas River and canyon slopes. It was the discovery of silver in 1632 that led to the founding of the town that soon grew into a service centre for the burgeoning mining industry. Vast amounts of silver were extracted over the next three centuries (some estimates say close to 100 million ounces), much of it transported almost 400 kilometres by mule train up the mountains and across the plains to Chihuahua. Mines in this area were believed to be among the richest in the world. The town developed an early hydroelectric plant, giving Batopilas the distinction of being the first place in the country outside Mexico City to have electricity. Some mining magnates used their fortunes to help the community install bridges, an aqueduct, and other improvements, while others preferred ostentatious displays of wealth. The oddest story is that of a mine owner in the 1700s who invited the bishop to come for a visit, then paved the street leading to the church with silver. Instead of being impressed, the bishop responded with a stern lecture on the evils of vanity.

While those glory days are long gone, the town still retains some of its architectural heritage, with restored colonial buildings and the ruins of a silver magnate's mansion. Walking into the old general store is like stepping back into another era, with spacious open shelves piled high with a hodgepodge of goods, and a worn wooden counter topped with an ancient cash register. We almost expect Pancho Villa to stroll in to pick up his groceries, or perhaps shoot up the place. Locals tell us one mainstay of the economy these days, unofficially at least, is marijuana production.

Travelling about eight kilometres from Batopilas along the river, we come to the isolated village of Satevo, home to the "lost cathedral" – a fairly elaborate Jesuit mission church from the 1700s, so-called partly because of its "middle of nowhere" location and its ambiguous origins. A fire destroyed all the records, leaving uncertainties as to exactly when it was built or why. Now famous for its postcard setting, the restored church overlooks the river with a backdrop of cactus-studded hills and canyon walls looking as though they've been painted shades of gold and red. Facts meld with myths, including an intriguing story of a lost treasure of the Sierra Madre. The King of Spain had expelled the Jesuits from Spanish territories in the 1760s, and the story goes that in their hasty departure, the successful and reputedly wealthy religious order left buried treasure somewhere in these hills.

Our travel mates are booked on the early afternoon train out of Creel, so we leave Batopilas just before sunrise. As we zigzag up the canyon slope, the rising sun transforms the rough rocky landscape, the warm glow making it softer and more inviting. There's no one else on the road, except for the surprise police checkpoint around a sharp curve. They're obviously on the lookout for drug runners who also use the route, so wave us through after a quick yet friendly "Buenos días". Plans call for paving the road all the way from Creel to Batopilas. It will certainly make the trip quicker and easier, but definitely bring more traffic and more tourists. As we bounce along the jagged rock pile road, where we seem to have this stunning countryside all to ourselves, we can't help but think that something will be lost as well.

After Creel, the next point heading west, as well as the highest station along the railway, is Divisadero. The train stops right beside a dramatic viewpoint overlooking the "divisadero", or dividing point, where three canyons meet. Names can be confusing, since this isn't just one distinct canyon, but a complex of canyons that all come together to form an enormous network that is several times larger, and deeper in places, than the Grand Canyon on the Colorado River. To add to the confusion, one of those canyons is named the Copper Canyon, but in common usage, the Copper Canyon name has also been adopted to refer to the entire canyon system.

Divisadero is normally a quiet spot, but four times a day it turns into crowded mayhem. Each trains stops for 20 minutes while passengers dash out for a quick look over the canyon. And anywhere in Mexico where there's a captive audience, there's bound to be food for sale. Food stalls line the railway tracks, with most cooking done on converted oil drums with built-in fire boxes. The flat top of the upturned barrel serves as a grill. At this stop, the most popular fast food offerings are "gorditas", thick tortillas stuffed with an assortment of fillings. It's almost like a 20-minute race for passengers – snap photos of the iconic vistas, look at the wares that the Tarahumara women have for sale, eat a gordita or two and grab an extra one for a later snack, then dash back aboard the waiting train. Of course, this is a prime spot to spend a couple days and do some exploring, something we save for later on the return leg of our trip.

We board the afternoon train for the long run to El Fuerte, arriving late at night. This is often the turn-around point for those doing the trip from the Chihuahua end, then returning. It's still 80 kilometres or so from the end of the line at Los Mochis, but we're now out of the canyon scenery. While El Fuerte is a pleasant colonial town, Los Mochis is a big city with a worsening reputation because of the drug war.

Since the eastbound train leaves early in the morning, we decide to spend two nights in El Fuerte. We choose a small hotel in the centre of town for no other reason than the bus to the train station stops across the street. Over breakfast the first morning, we chat with the friendly couple running the hotel. Owner Enrique asks us what we have planned for the day. When we tell him not much, he says that he'll be spending the afternoon relaxing at his place by the lake. He needs a day off, and invites us to tag along. His handyman, Miguel, is also coming to do a few jobs.

Our first stop on the way out of town is to pick up beer – lots of beer – and an assortment of peanuts and other snacks. Part way out of town, they realize that they forgot to buy limes. Apparently, it's unthinkable to eat peanuts without the customary squeeze of lime juice. "Don't worry," announces Miguel, as he directs Enrique along a minor road in the suburbs where he just happens to know of a lime tree with branches full of fruit conveniently draping over the road.

We aren't sure what to expect at this "place by the lake". It turns out to be a simple tool shed on a gravelly knoll, with no trees, and the lake in the distance. Not the most appealing spot at first glance, but Enrique sees great potential. Building of the dam on the El Fuerte River created a reservoir, and long narrow lots bordering the water had been subdivided and sold. As far as we could see, not a lot of development has taken place.

Enrique pulled folding lawn chairs out of the tool shed, and set them up on the shady side. Here we sat for most of the afternoon, drinking beer and eating peanuts (with lime, of course), while chatting about whatever came to mind; a good workout for our Spanish.

Miguel did do a bit of work. A pile of gravel about 10 metres away had to be moved, for whatever reason, closer to the shed. In the hot noon-day sun, Miguel shovels gravel into the wheelbarrow, dumps it on the new pile, then retreats to the shade to take it easy and drink beer. Sufficiently rested and refreshed, he moves another wheelbarrow full, then heads to the shade for more rest and more beer. This pattern continues for the next couple hours until most of the gravel has been moved and most of the beer is gone.

Enrique tells us about his ambitious plans – building a cabin, getting a boat, and maybe starting a sport fishing business; the bass fishing is said to be quite good. But judging by how fast things are happening, there doesn't seem to be any great hurry. We get the impression that the simple pleasures of the here and now are every bit as important to him – just having a quiet getaway where he can sit in the shade of a tool shed, sip his favourite brew, munch on peanuts (with lime, of course), and dream about possibilities.

The eastbound train leaves early next morning, allowing us to enjoy the best part of the train journey, the section that we missed travelling in the dark on the westbound trip. It isn't long before we leave the coastal plains, enter thick forest and rocky foothills, and soon cross the El Fuerte River. The engine grunts and groans as we slowly but constantly gain altitude. Out the window one eye-popping scene passes after another with a succession of mountains, lakes, valleys, tunnels, bridges, rivers, and gorges. The train slows to a crawl as we cross the Çhinipas River. Leaning out the open window between the cars, we look straight down at the water over 100 metres below. The highlight of this section comes near the village of Temoris, where towering vertical cliffs and waterfalls line the deep valley. A series of spirals take us climbing ever higher, first making a U-turn on a bridge across the river valley, then completing another 180-degree turn through a tunnel inside the mountain. At one point, we can see three different levels of railway track.

We bought our ticket as far as the Posada Barrancas station, near the small town of Areponapuchi (Arepo for short), and just five kilometres from the next stop at Divisadero. The train lets us off at the platform then immediately pulls away; we're the only ones leaving the train. After walking the half kilometre or so down the lonely dusty road into the village, we find a simple motel-like room in a guesthouse. It's clear that this place is a work in progress. Other rooms are in various stages of completion, to be finished we later learn, when finances allow. We're the only guests.

The owner, Rojelio, drops by in the evening after a long day's work. Like many people here, he's a jack-of-all-trades, and does what he has to do in order to make a living. Mainly, he is an artisan, making jewelry and crafts that he sells to tourists. His specialty is copper bracelets, a nice tie-in with the name of the canyon. Never mind that the canyon name was derived from the copper colour of sunlit cliffs rather than the metal. Most days he follows a circuit, setting up his wares based on the train's schedule and tours from nearby hotels, then rushing back home to take care of the guest-house. Rojelio's wife balances raising their five children with duties at the guesthouse, such as cooking our breakfast, then sometimes takes the short drive to Divisadero station to help her mother who runs a food stall making gorditas for passengers.

From Arepo, it's not far to the canyon rim with magnificent views. Another 20 minutes or so along the scenic path and we arrive at Divisadero. Along the way we pass the famous Posada Barrancas Mirador Hotel, that literally clings to the cliff face, with balconies looking straight down into the canyon. Visitors spending the night either stay at one of the few first class hotels nearby, or in Arepo. Our village accommodation lacks the view, but comes at a fraction of the price, plus there's the added bonus of getting to know local people such as Rojelio and his family.

Everywhere we go it's one dynamite view after another. At one spot on the rim, an observation deck juts out from the clifftop, its floor made of clear plexiglas so that you peer straight down into the abyss. The sensation is almost like floating in the air suspended high above the canyon floor. If you're exceptionally brave, or totally lacking in sanity, you can try your luck on the balancing rock right on the cliff's edge. The idea is to rock the boulder back and forth, which looks like it could topple over the edge, but never does...at least not yet.

More paths lead into the forest through stands of distinctive Apache pine, its wispy yet strong needles growing up to a foot long. A labyrinth of other trails wind down into the canyon, dotted with isolated Tarahumara buildings and cave dwellings.

As we walk back to Rojelio's guesthouse in late afternoon, the tourists are gone and the last souvenir hawkers are packing up for the day. The low sun just clears the rim of the canyon, flooding the multicoloured cliffs with bright bronze and coppery tones. Canyon depths fall into shadow while the pure light illuminates the hilltops. We're so glad that we allowed ourselves more than just the 20-minute train stop.

All Aflutter in Mexico

The Great Monarch Migration

Monarch butterfly at El Rosario.

It's warm under the big stack of blankets, but the air in our room is crisp and cool. Like many buildings in the small mountain town of Angangueo, our hotel has no heating. The evening before we sat in our room wearing sweaters and jackets and drinking plenty of hot tea to ward off the mid-January chill. Now we have to get up so that we can head even higher into the mountains, to about 10,000 feet or close to 3,000 metres, where it's even colder. But once we remember where we are, thoughts of cold are quickly replaced with anticipation of what awaits. We've come to see one of nature's most unusual and awesome displays.

Monarch butterflies in North America have two important over-wintering sites. Those west of the Rocky Mountains head to the California coast, while those east of the Rockies – spread over an enormous chunk of Canada and the United States – head to a relatively small area of forested mountain tops in the Mexican state of Michoacán, west of Mexico City. The butterflies have been coming here every winter for who knows how long. Surprisingly, it wasn't until 1975 that researchers finally discovered the long unanswered mystery of where the monarchs go. Local people around Angangueo always knew they were here, but when you have always lived with butterflies, why would you think that this is anything unusual? They're not taken for granted anymore. Today, the Monarch Butterfly Biosphere Reserve is a UNESCO World Heritage Site.

The monarchs arrive in late November and early December and stay until sometime in March. Their numbers vary; in a good year it can be in the hundreds of millions. This area offers protection in a forest canopy of primarily oyamel fir trees, nearby sources of water, and a cool climate where they can preserve their energy. Unfortunately, their choice of a place that is often just above freezing puts them in a delicate balance, and every once in a while Mother Nature throws them for a loop. Frost is bad news and the occasional snowstorm can be disastrous. During the unusually harsh winter of 2002, over half the population died.

Our journey starts with a three-hour bus ride from Mexico City to the city of Zitácuaro, where we transfer to a local bus that winds slowly up the mountains, past corn fields and villages for another hour to Angangueo. The entire contingent of guests staying at our hotel – a family of five from Mexico City, a woman from Germany, and us – gets together to hire a van and driver to take us up to El Rosario, one of the most accessible of the nearby monarch reserves.

Finding someone to take us is easy. In fact, they find us. New faces in town are easy to spot, and we seldom walk more than a block down the narrow cobblestone streets without someone stopping to ask if we want to see the "mariposas".

The four-wheel drive van crawls slowly up the rough gravel road, along a series of switchbacks taking us ever higher with sweeping views of the valley far below. At the entrance to the reserve a local guide leads us on a footpath to a semi-open area in the forest where the butterflies hang out – literally hang out. At first it's difficult to realize what we are looking at; it seems that many of the trees have trunks and branches twice their normal thickness.

"It's all butterflies," whispers our guide in Spanish.

Normally a bold orange, monarchs are a more muted brownish gold when roosting with their wings folded. We're looking at layer upon layer of butterflies clinging to trees. We came early in the morning because, in theory, we would see this phenomenon while it is still cool, then as the sun warms the air, the butterflies would emerge from the trees and we would see them fly off to feed and water.

But Mother Nature throws us for a loop as well. It's one of those mornings that weather forecasters like to call a mix of sun and cloud. The sun never stays out for more than three or four minutes before another cloud comes by. The brief warmth stirs a few monarchs off the branches and into the sky, but then a cloud immediately brings them back to roost. The temperature is apparently right on the borderline between what they consider warm or cold. It stays like that for the next couple hours, never warming enough for many butterflies to leave the security of the branches.

By the time we arrive back in town, the mix of sun and cloud turns to pounding rain. We decide to stay another day, in hopes that the weather will improve. Walking around town in the evening after the rain storm ends, we meet Diego, another of the many locals who offer transport to the reserves. We talk about another reserve, Sierra Chincua, which is slightly farther away from Angangueo, and arrange for an early morning pick-up, assuming the weather cooperates.

The following morning is crisp but clear as we head up into the hills of Sierra Chincua. At the entrance to the reserve at the end of the road, we have the choice of either walking or hiring horses to reach the viewing area. Since it is uphill at an altitude near 10,000 feet, we allow ourselves the luxury of riding up the dusty path.

Leaving the horses, our guide Arturo leads us along the heavily forested path to a ridge that slopes into the valley below. Before long we come to a clump of trees thick with butterflies; many are already flying around as the mid-morning sun warms the forest. We stare at the spectacular sight, content to just stay there and watch, but Arturo assures us that just a little farther on, it gets even better. By this time we shed jackets and sweaters as it feels more like a summer than a January day.

The monarchs react to the warmth as well. Soon the semi-dormant butterflies come to life and take to the air by the thousands, then tens of thousands, perhaps hundreds of thousands; there's so many it's hard to tell. Bold splashes of orange speckle the blue sky as countless monarch butterflies fill the air and land on branches, logs, the ground, even on our heads and shoulders. We move slowly and carefully so as not to step on any. The sound is unlike anything we have heard before – a gentle, whispering-like whir, like a million pieces of confetti thrown in the air. Awestruck visitors speak in hushed tones as we witness the breathtaking spectacle.

Arturo talks in Spanish about the monarch migration, and

shows us an easy way to tell males from females – males have a couple of extra black spots on their wings.

This migration is unique. No other butterfly in the world migrates this far and in such great numbers. The distance they travel from some parts of Canada can be as much as 5,000 kilometres. Their travels have been likened to bird migrations, but with a twist. Individual butterflies make the one-way journey only once, and many don't survive the long trip. No monarch lives long enough to make a round trip, so no single butterfly can "remember" the route. The ones that make the return journey the following year might be the grandkids or even the great grandkids of this year's migrants. Exactly how they find their way is still a mystery.

Threats to monarchs come from many fronts, the most obvious being shrinking habitat and deforestation. Key parts of the forest have been set aside as wildlife reserves, but there is constant pressure from logging interests and even illegal logging. In remote sectors of some reserves, armed rangers patrol looking for illegal loggers. On a positive note, the increased attention to the monarchs has helped the local economy, long dependent on mining and subsistence farming. Most tourist services, from guides in the reserves, to people providing transport, food, and lodging are run by locals. They have seen how the monarchs have contributed to their livelihood, and have become some of the strongest voices for conservation.

Altering habitats in Canada and the United States are also having an effect. Monarchs are picky eaters – the caterpillars dine exclusively on milkweed which contains chemicals that are poisonous to most birds. A bird that decides to eat a monarch soon regrets its menu selection. The bright orange colour has developed as a way of warning birds, "Eat me and you'll be sorry!" But milkweed is often in short supply, and one cause that scientists point to is the increasing use of genetically modified crops that are herbicide resistant. Spraying a field to kill everything but the crop may be an efficient way of controlling weeds, but this also means less food for butterflies. The wild card in the longer term may be global warming which could alter the time of year that milkweed and other plants flower, adding to the many challenges that monarchs already face.

We leave with a feeling of exhilaration from seeing one of the great marvels of nature. But that feeling is tempered with the realization that this is a marvel teetering on the edge.

THE WINDS OF PATAGONIA
Glaciers, Guanacos, and Gales Galore

Guanaco at Torres del Paine National Park, Chile.

Just outside El Calafate we stop to take a photo of the world's most redundant highway sign, a picture of a tree half bent over, reminding us that it could be windy. As if we need reminding. The car continues to rock and shudder in the howling gale. Before getting out, we remember the stern warning from the car rental lady. "Always open the door slowly. Always firmly with both hands."

Patagonia leaves us with rich memories of magnificent mountains, imposing glaciers, wild coastlines, green fertile valleys, and gauchos tending sheep and cattle on wide open plains. But what really sticks in our minds is the wind, not simply a weather condition in Patagonia, but an integral part of the landscape. The wide contrast in temperature from Antarctica to the south and the tropics to the north makes the latitudes between 40 and 50 degrees south some of the windiest places on Earth. Sailors dubbed it the Roaring 40s.

This is roughly where we find Patagonia, covering about the southern third of the land mass of Argentina and Chile, but with only around five per cent of their people. Patagonia is as much an idea as a place. It isn't a country, since it straddles two nations often at odds with each other as to where the border runs. It isn't even a distinct geographical or political division. Argentinian Patagonia is generally thought of as the land south of the Rio Negro, a river that slices through the province of Rio Negro. The northern extent of Patagonia in Chile is fairly nebulous, somewhere in the neighbourhood of the 40th parallel. Yet the mere mention of Patagonia evokes visions of what this place is, a land defined by vastness, remoteness, and wildness – the quintessential landscape of the mind.

A three-hour flight from Buenos Aires brings us to El Calafate, a rapidly growing tourist town in the southwest corner of Argentina. Its prime location makes it a popular jumping-off point to explore southern Patagonia, with less than a two-hour drive to one of the world's most famous glaciers, and drives of less than a day, in opposite directions, to Patagonia's two most iconic landmarks – Mount Fitzroy and Torres del Paine.

Owing entirely to luck rather than planning, we arrive in El Calafate just in time for the annual rodeo, attracting competitors from throughout southern Argentina and neighbouring parts of Chile. The main event is riding, or rather attempting to ride, bucking horses. Facilities are simple – a post in the middle of the field where reluctant horses are led then tied up. The rider saddles up, gets on, then at the signal, the horse is untied with the sudden yank of the rope. The mayhem begins as the violently bucking horse takes the rider on a gyrating roller coaster course, usually ending with the rider biting the dust. Between events a poet recites passionate lyrics on the life and struggles of the gaucho.

The event is not only about riding well, but also about looking good. While some competitors wear non-descript work clothes, many don classic gaucho garb – baggy pants tucked into high boots, wide decorated belt holding an ornate knife, a beret or a wide-brimmed, almost pancake-flat hat. Most surprising is the choice of footwear. We would expect that getting thrashed around by a horse would call for those substantial-looking high gaucho boots, but many riders wear simple pieces of leather on their feet, held by laces tied around the ankles.

Heading west of El Calafate, we follow the shore of Lago Argentino, its waters a brilliant turquoise blue from melted glacial ice. Heading into the mountains, we enter Los Glaciares National Park, recognized as a UNESCO World Heritage Site. We know that we're getting close to world-famous Perito Moreno Glacier, but when we round a corner and see it for the first time, it still takes us by surprise.

Everything about it is on a grand scale, covering 250 square kilometres, 30 kilometres long, and with a five-kilometre-wide terminus. One of 47 major glaciers extending down from the largest ice cap in the world outside the polar regions, Perito Moreno isn't even the biggest one. What makes it special is the unparalleled setting and easy access. We can walk almost right up to it. Paths and boardwalks provide a variety of spectacular views, but the highlight is taking a boat trip on the lake where we approach the glacier's leading edge and stare up at the imposing 70-metre-high wall of fractured ice.

Perito Moreno is an exception to most of the world's glaciers which are receding, many very quickly. Until the 1990s, Perito Moreno was described as one of few glaciers in the world that was still advancing. Today, it is often referred to as being "in equilibrium"; it advances about two metres per day, but loses its mass at about the same rate. We hear the expansive tongue of ice groaning and cracking as pieces of the face fall away, sending towering shafts of age-old ice crashing into Lago Argentino as the glacier "calves". Every so often, enormous chunks break away in a thunderous roar, as icebergs collapse into the lake, creating powerful waves and sending spray skyward.

While Perito Moreno is considered southern Patagonia's most famous "must see", this certainly isn't the place to get a sense of the remote and lonely Patagonia of legend. By late afternoon, the entrance gates and viewing areas become so crowded that park staff have to direct traffic in the parking lot.

Instead of following the throngs back to El Calafate at the end of the day, we take a minor road along the southern arm of Lago Argentino to Lago Roca, a remote mountain lake just back from the main lake. We settle into a campground at this quiet spot for a couple of nights. While only a short drive from Perito Moreno, and still in the midst of impressive landscapes, it seems a world away. The crowds are gone; the small number of campers are either fishing or hiking in the hills. We wander through rolling grassy hills scattered with wildflowers next to the peaceful lake where fly fishermen cast for trout. The lake is backed by magnificent mountains where lush forests give way to snow-capped peaks. Views from hilltops look over a wider country of peaks, glaciers, and turquoise waters.

It's difficult to leave this idyllic spot, but we're beckoned by another Patagonian icon. Heading north, we pass the eastern edge of Lago Argentino, cross wide open tablelands, then skirt the shores of Lago Viedma, its glacial waters an equally dazzling blue. The approach to El Chalten ranks among the most dramatic of any town, anywhere. The dusty tourist town lies nestled at the very foot of Mount Fitzroy, the symbol of Argentinian Patagonia. The majestic mountain complex has two peaks considered among the most difficult in the world to climb – the main Cerro Fitzroy at 3,405 metres, and Cerro Torre (the Tower) at 3,128 metres. The mountain was named for Captain Fitzroy of the HMS *Beagle*, the British ship that explored and mapped much of southern Patagonia in the 1830s, one of its crew being a young Charles Darwin.

El Chalten is so new that it wasn't even founded until 1985, established primarily to preempt claims by Chile, which lies just over the mountain tops. The town may be dusty when the inevitable winds whip up dust devils and fierce gales, but what a location! Billed as the Trekking Capital of Argentina, magnificent hiking trails abound – everything from day trips to multi-day excursions lie literally out our back door.

The day we start our overnight hike to the foot of Cerro Fitzroy, something is unusual. No wind; a strange but welcome respite from the daily blast we've come to expect. We walk along hilly slopes, through forest, along mountain streams, most of the way enjoying stunning views of the peaks, which keep getting closer and closer. When we arrive at the campsite overlooking the base of the peak, several campers are already there. This is by far the most popular backcountry campsite in this region of Los Glaciares National Park, and by evening close to a hundred tents have sprung up. After a quick camp walk-through, we estimate that perhaps half the hikers are Argentinian. Judging by the mix of Spanish, Portuguese, German, French, English, Dutch and other languages we hear, the other half seems to come from all over the world.

Our hope is to photograph sunrise on the mountain peaks. But as all photographers know, changing weather can make short work of the best laid plans. It doesn't look promising due to heavy cloud cover. Then by dusk the sun breaks through just enough to light up the clouds behind the mountain peaks, making for a spectacular sunset. Next morning we rise well before daybreak to find a gloriously clear sky. As the sun begins to come up, the stark rocky spires of Fitzroy start to warm, while the surrounding landscape remains in darkness. Then over the next five minutes or so, the magical transformation takes place, as the peaks turn a brilliant, almost unreal red, as if they're on fire.

While Mount Fitzroy is the iconic symbol for Argentinian Patagonia, for Chile it is Torres del Paine, our next destination. We return to El Calafate, then head south, crossing the high plains to the border with Chile, then down the lonely road to the national park. We can see the lofty spires of Torres del Paine a long way before reaching the park, distinct and separated from the main Andes range. Although we enjoy a clear blue sky on our drive, we know things will be changing shortly when we see ominous clouds crowning the towers. It would stay this way for days, almost as if the clouds were permanently tethered to the peaks. These mountains are so huge that they create their own weather patterns.

By the time we reach the entrance to Torres del Paine National Park, a storm has developed, shrouding the landscape in low clouds, cold drizzling rain, and ferocious winds. In the distance we see what looks like an isolated rainstorm below the low clouds. But something is odd – this "rainstorm" doesn't have a top. As we get closer and pull over beside one of the bigger lakes, it's apparent that the water is going up, not down! Violent winds whip up waves, and gusts pick up the crests, sending spray high into the air.

We're planning to camp, not an appealing prospect in this weather. But we're pleasantly surprised to find that each campsite has its own compact shelter with a roof and walls on two sides to offer at least some protection from the elements. And talk about a room with a view. Sitting on the edge of Lago Pehoe, we look over an unobstructed view of the mountain, from this side dominated by the Cuernos del Paine (the Horns of Paine), massive, smooth granite cliffs that look like horns. We have visions of being able to watch the rising sun light up the mountain every morning. However, both sun and clouds prove less than cooperative. It's not until our fourth morning at this spot that the sun finally peeks through the shroud of clouds on the towers for a few precious moments, illuminating the slopes of the horns in a golden glow. Then it's over; the crown of swirling clouds closes in again, turning the sky that familiar steely grey.

It rains a lot, with unrelenting winds. The first morning we wake up to damp sleeping bags and a wet floor in the tent. We're surprised because this trusty tent has kept us dry in all kinds of storms. It doesn't take long to find the problem – the tent is designed to deflect rain coming from above, not from below. The sustained wind was so strong that it blew the falling rain into the small space between the fly of the tent and the ground.

It's the hiking that brings many people to Torres del Paine. In addition to the major circuit around the mountain, and the popular multi-day W-hike (so named because the route is shaped like a "W"), there are several choices in day walks. We let the weather govern how much hiking we do. One pleasant walk starts right behind the campsite, but closer to the top ridge, the fierce wind makes it almost impossible to even stand upright. We later learn that the winds we're experiencing are worse than normal, which doesn't surprise us. Other hikers in the park at that time cancelled their hikes because of the real possibility of being blown off the cliff.

Having a car saves the day. The park has a fairly extensive road network, so even in bad weather, we are able to explore and photograph the lakes with impossibly blue glacial water, glaciers, river torrents, waterfalls, and viewpoints galore. Wildlife takes the weather in stride. Majestic Andean condors with three-metre wingspans continue to soar through the sky. The national bird of Chile, this black vulture looks as if it's wearing a white collar. Rheas, ostrich-like flightless birds, wander open grassy areas. Though more at home on the plains than in the mountains, those we come across appear relaxed, probably knowing that they're protected. Our biggest surprise is seeing brilliant pink flamingos wading in shallow lakes. While we usually associate them with more tropical climes, Chilean flamingos often summer in mountainous areas.

The critter that really defines Torres del Paine is the guanaco, a wild cousin of the llama and the largest wild land mammal in South America. A beautiful tan to dark cinnamon colour, they have long necks, split upper lips like camels (which they are related to), and big saucer-like eyes with showy eyelashes. They walk on padded feet with toenails rather than hooves.

Throughout our travels in southern Patagonia, we see the occasional guanaco, but nothing like here. The resurgence in their once dwindling population is one of the park's great success stories. Now they are so common that a herd sometimes takes over the road, and we have to either wait for them to move on, or slowly inch our way through. Getting close for photos is never an issue. We stop at a hilltop overlooking Lago Nordenskjöld to take photos of the awesome setting with towering cliffs looming over the glacial lake. A guanaco wanders to the top of a ridge and looks over the edge of the lake, as if we had willed it to head to that particular spot to complete the picture. If only more wildlife would be that considerate to photographers.

While we're this far south, we decide to drive the additional 500 kilometres or so all the way to the southern tip of the South American mainland. We arrive at Puerto Natales, a little over 100 kilometres from the park, where we have our first glimpse of the sea. The town sits on ominously named Seno Ultima Esperanza (Last Hope Sound), named by Spanish Captain Juan Ladrillero in 1557, while trying to find his way through the maze of islands and bays in the Straits of Magellan. This bay was his last hope at discovering the route, and unfortunately it wasn't the right choice.

The town was founded as a port for the sheep industry, but now it is better known as a jumping-off point for visits to Torres del Paine. Today, its seaport serves as the southern terminus for a four-day ferry trip north to Puerto Montt. The route runs through the Chilean fjords, a complex of rugged and remote islands bordering the Pacific, known for stormy weather. We had booked passage on the ship before leaving for South America, but it was not to be. Two weeks before our departure date, the trip was cancelled because the ship had suffered severe damage in a storm and was grounded for repair.

Just outside Puerto Natales, we stop at the most unusual shrine we have come across anywhere. Right beside the highway, hundreds of plastic Coca-Cola, Fanta, and other pop bottles are neatly stacked against simple wooden shrines to Difunta Correa, a legendary though unofficial saint. A handwritten sign says "Gracias por ayudarme" – thank you for helping me. The story goes that in the 19th century, a woman was crossing the desert in Argentina with her infant baby, ran out of water, and died of thirst. Gauchos herding cattle found her body, but were astonished to discover that the baby was still alive, feeding from the mother's breasts which were still miraculously full of milk. Though not recognized by the church, Correa is believed to perform miracles, so shrines like this have been built in various parts of southern Argentina and Chile. Leaving bottles assures that she will never be thirsty again.

We leave the mountains, and after crossing scenic rolling hills and valleys, home to sprawling sheep and cattle ranches, we get our first glance of the Straits of Magellan. Mapped by Portuguese explorer Ferdinand Magellan in 1520, the famous navigation route between the Atlantic and Pacific takes ships through a protected course between the mainland and a hodgepodge of islands, the biggest being Tierra del Fuego.

Before continuing down the main highway along the shore of the strait, we take a detour to Otway Sound, only a few kilometres across the narrow neck of the mainland. On a barren windswept shore, we find a wildlife refuge protecting a colony of Magellanic penguins. These mid-sized penguins, little more than a half metre tall, have mostly black and white plumage, with pinkish face patches. Also called jackass penguins for their strange call that sounds like a braying donkey, they breed only in the southern part of South America and the Falkland Islands.

We follow a pathway winding through the nesting area where they dig shallow burrows into the sandy soil. They pretty much ignore us as they go about their business, occasionally peeking out to check for danger. Another path leads to the water's edge where the penguins come ashore after feeding in the sea. We don't stay long; the relentless wind chills us to the bone with gusts so forceful that we're sandblasted by coarse grains of sand. Several penguins take it all in stride, simply hanging out and standing around on the wind-battered shoreline. Just another day at the beach for these tough birds.

We soon arrive at Punta Arenas, the largest centre in the region, and the southernmost major city in the world. Built on sheep farming and as a means of asserting Chile's sovereignty over the strait, Punta Arenas thrived as a supply centre for the shipping route around the bottom of South America. Its fortunes diminished considerably when the Panama Canal opened in 1914. Agriculture still remains important, along with fishing, oil and gas exploration, and a growing tourism industry.

The city centre has several reminders of the glory days, with mansions built by wool barons, and European neo-classical buildings around the centre square dominated by a statue of Ferdinand Magellan. Most intriguing is the cemetery, where treed walkways are lined with grandiose, highly ornate mausoleums for the rich and famous. We drive up to the viewpoint at Cerro de la Cruz to look over the sprawling city of 150,000 spread along the shoreline, with Tierra del Fuego far on the horizon. The city looks more colourful from up here. Most houses have metal roofs, with an array of bright green, red, blue, and bronze.

Punta Arenas is not quite at the southern end of the mainland, so we decide to see how far we can go. This last section of road that passes small fishing communities has a rich history. Fort Bulnes is a reconstructed wooden fort where Chile took possession of the Strait in 1843 and established its first Patagonian village. While the fort was well situated for defence, the inhospitable climate and lack of arable land for agriculture made it a poor choice for settlement. After years of struggle, they moved the settlement 60 kilometres farther north to Punta Arenas.

Nearby, a monument commemorates an early 16th century settlement that also resulted in failure, but with more serious consequences. In 1584, the Spanish tried to establish a colony, but almost everyone died of hunger. It became known as Puerto del Hambre, or Port Famine.

Another tragedy comes to light in the nearby English Cemetery where many Scottish settlers were buried over the years. The oldest marker takes us back to the first voyage of the HMS *Beagle* in 1828, and the death of its captain, Commander Pringle Stokes. The epitaph on the cross above his grave says that he died "from the effects of the anxieties and hardships while surveying the western shores of Tierra del Fuego". What it doesn't say is that he shot himself. It wasn't until the second voyage of the *Beagle* that the survey was completed, under the command of Captain Fitzroy, accompanied by the soon-to-be famous naturalist, Charles Darwin.

At Punta Santa Ana, a sign reads "Fin Continente Americano" – the end of the American continent. Though North and South America are called separate continents, both make up one continuous chunk of land, divided only by an artificial canal in Panama. So technically it would be possible to walk all the way from our home in Canada to this point without ever leaving land, other than crossing the odd bridge. Strictly speaking, the official southernmost tip is Cabo Froward, just slightly south of Punta Santa Ana, past the end of the road. The road continues a few kilometres, then deteriorates into a minor trail following the very edge of the water. We turn around, content that we've come close enough to the bottom of the continent.

Strangely, Chile considers Punta Santa Ana to be the geographic centre of the country. The reasoning is that this is exactly half way between Chile's northern border and the South Pole. Chile claims a pie-shaped piece of Antarctica, starting at the South Pole. This overlaps with claims also made by Argentina and Britain, none of which are recognized internationally.

Turning north, we follow the wide Straits of Magellan until we cross back to Argentina near the Atlantic coast. We decide to head to Monte León National Park, about 300 kilometres north, in part because guidebooks call it "little-visited". Most of the way we follow Highway #3, the country's main north-south link, running a bit inland from the sea, crossing broad grassland plains where we can see forever.

At the turnoff to Monte León, still about 20 kilometres away on the coast, we find the gate to the access road locked. So we go to the Guardaparque (park ranger) office to see what's going on. It had rained hard the day before, one of the rangers explains, making the gravel and dirt road impassable. But with today's strong sunshine and ever-present howling winds, he figures that by mid-afternoon it should be dry enough to open the gate.

To pass the time, we take a short drive up the highway to Puerto Santa Cruz, near the estuary of the Santa Cruz River. Starting some 400 kilometres away at glacier-fed Lago Argentino, the mighty river flows from the edge of the Andes, through boundless

Patagonian plains, and eventually to the Atlantic. When the *Beagle* came here in 1832, Captain Fitzroy tried to explore upriver using small boats. Much of the arduous 21-day journey was spent dragging the boats upstream. They did manage to make it close to the mountains, but were forced to turn back when the rapids became impossible to negotiate. Darwin's journal talks about how they "viewed these grand mountains with regret." Captain Fitzroy would never set foot on the mountain to be named after him.

The only remarkable part of Puerto Santa Cruz is the statue that greets us on the way in. Most South American towns are fond of monuments to great battles and great generals, but here we find a huge statue of Santa Claus. Instead of a sleigh and reindeer, he is riding in a chariot pulled by guanacos.

The park gate is open when we return, and we drive down the just barely dry narrow road that gets steep at the end as we descend through badland-like hills toward the weather-beaten shore. Ominous-looking storm clouds build around us; we wonder how long the roads will stay dry. No other traffic is around, then eventually a four-wheel drive truck pulls up – it's the park ranger we had met earlier at the office. As we stop for a chat, the clouds suddenly open up in a ferocious downpour, complete with pelting hail. We look at the muddy roads and think about making it back up the hill.

"I don't know when you will be able to get out," he says.

We'll worry about that later. In the meantime we can still drive the mostly level roads near the coast. The windswept shoreline is lined with cliffs, many sculpted with holes and caves from the constantly pounding surf. Some caves near shore are accessible if you time your visit carefully during low tide. These are especially high tides, about 35 feet or 10 metres, forming wide tidepools and beaches. Walking along the shore, we find numerous fossils in the rocks, especially perfectly formed sea shells. One promontory rising from the sea is the source of the park's name – Monte León, or Lion Mount. Use your imagination and squint your eyes just right, and it sorta-kinda looks like a reclining lion with its head up.

The real wildlife is more interesting. Guanacos and rheas wander the hills, sea lions frequent the shoreline rocks, and colonies of cormorants nest on rocky islands right next to the shore. A brazen Patagonian fox stays near our campsite, probably looking for a handout. It's a beautiful animal with a coat of reddish grey, about intermediate in size between a red fox and a coyote.

But what we enjoy most are the penguins – the world's fourth largest Magellanic penguin colony, with an estimated 150,000 birds. From a clifftop viewpoint, we watch them waddle out of the water in early evening, then make the long, arduous climb uphill to their nests among low, inhospitable-looking thorny bushes. A marked walking trail winds through the nesting colony; we're so close to the birds that they're almost within reach. The experience is way more rewarding than seeing the penguins at Otway, and here we have them all to ourselves.

It seems that we pretty much have the whole park to ourselves. A couple other vehicles drive through during the day, but in the evening, we are alone in the campground. This little-visited park has only the most rudimentary facilities, but we certainly can't complain – we don't have to pay park admission fees or even camping fees.

The last major stop before heading back to El Calafate, Monte León turns out to be a fitting end to our southern Patagonia wanderings. While the mountain parks have more obvious grandeur, being alone in this wild and remote place really gives us a feel for the immensity of this special land.

As for getting back up that hill we were worried about – no problem at all. Thanks to the sun and our constant companion, the Patagonian wind.

VOYAGE TO THE BOTTOM OF THE WORLD
Exploring the Antarctic Peninsula

Rocks, ice, and snow of Antarctica.

"It's time to Drake proof your cabins," cautions Brook, the ship's expedition leader. "Take everything that you don't want to break and put it on the floor, because that's where it will end up anyway."

We're aboard the P/V *Mariya Yermolova*, a small Russian ship specially fitted for ice conditions, bound for Antarctica. Leaving the port of Ushuaia, Argentina's most southerly town, we cruise the protected waters of the Beagle Channel in late evening, and round Cape Horn at the tip of South America.

Now we're about to experience the "Drake Shake," two days of wave-induced roller coaster rides across the infamous Drake

Passage, until we enter the quieter waters of the South Shetland Islands. The thousand-kilometre-wide passage is named for Sir Francis Drake, who was accidentally caught in these turbulent waters when storms pushed his ship far south of the Cape and left him floundering in fierce gales. The seas here are considered the stormiest and roughest in the world, due primarily to the Antarctic Convergence where warm waters of the Atlantic and Pacific Oceans meet cold surface waters that encircle Antarctica.

For the next 48 hours or so, *Mariya Yermolova* rocks and rolls while our stomachs do much the same. We manage to make it to all the meals, but many do not. After the first couple sittings we remember not to put our elbows on the table. Not that we have impeccable manners; it's to avoid getting wet. In rough seas, tablecloths are put on wet to keep plates and food from sliding around, a simple technique that works incredibly well. If only we could keep ourselves from sliding around. Most passengers walk like drunks on a long weekend bender, leaning left, leaning right, grabbing handrails, and trying to avoid – not always successfully – running into walls or other people.

Out on the back deck where there's some protection from the wind, we grasp onto railings extra tightly. Raging seas aren't enough to deter Marco, the ship's bird expert, from leading us outside to see what's flying around. Even these remote stormy seas have signs of life, including birds such as storm petrels, giant petrels, and royal albatross. The most awesome sight is the big daddy of them all, the wandering albatross, with the widest wingspan of any bird in the world – over three metres on average, with some stretching even more. Flying low, they effortlessly cruise the wind currents just above the waves, rarely flapping their wings. As the name suggests, they wander far and wide, covering thousands of kilometres and staying at sea practically non-stop. They head for land every two years to breed in nesting colonies on isolated islands.

The second day into the crossing, we're feeling reasonably proud of the way we're handling the Drake Shake. After all, we haven't thrown up or broken any bones yet, although that queasy feeling is almost always there. But when we ask one of the crew how this compares with other crossings, he bursts our bubble by saying, "This isn't too bad at all. I've seen a lot worse."

Many of the other 100 or so passengers are well-travelled. But while they may have "been there, done that" in a big chunk of the world, everyone agrees that Antarctica stands in a class by itself. Although travel to the white continent has increased in recent years, it is still looked upon as a once-in-a-lifetime journey to a mostly unknown land at the bottom of the world that is both foreboding and wildly alluring. We laugh when we hear that most of us have much the same story. Tell people that we're going to Antarctica, and the response tends to be one of two extremes – "Wow, is that ever cool," or "Why in the world would you want to go there?"

We settle into the ship's casual atmosphere. The bridge is almost always open to visitors, where Captain Sviridov and his crew patiently explain routings, map readings, and the dazzling array of instruments and gizmos with blinking lights. While the ship is sailing, we can choose from among a series of presentations on everything to do with Antarctica: geography, wildlife, politics, the Antarctic Treaty, and famous explorers such as Scott and Amundsen who raced to be the first to the South Pole.

To say that the expedition leaders know their stuff would be an understatement. Brian, from the United States, spent much of his career in Antarctica, including running the U.S. McMurdo Antarctic Research Station. Adam, from Sweden, is a marine mammal expert.

Marco is an Argentine biologist who spent two years at an Antarctic research station studying for his Ph.D. in Antarctic birds. Want to know some intricate detail about penguin behaviour? Marco can tell you. He debunks the commonly held belief that penguins mate for life.

"Penguins mate for a long time, but it can get complicated," he explains. "It's like people who also supposedly mate for life. But as we know, that gets complicated too."

Just as we're starting to become accustomed to the Drake Shake, we enter the protected waters of the South Shetland Islands, about 120 kilometres off the tip of the Antarctic Peninsula. Near Aitcho Island, we board rubber Zodiacs for our first landing at our first of many penguin colonies. Thousands of gentoo penguins occupy nests spreading across the gently sloping land between the high hills and the stony beach, their incessant braying-like calls interrupted by occasional snorts and grunts of elephant seals. The penguins ignore us, and if we stand still in one spot, some even approach out of curiosity. Averaging around .75 metres or about 2.5 feet tall, with a distinctive orange bill and white head patch, gentoos look rather awkward as they waddle around. All that changes when they hit the water, where they are considered the fastest swimmers of any birds in the world, capable of bursts of speed over 25 km/hour.

Over the ridge we find a colony of chinstrap penguins. These black and white birds have a thin black line across the lower part of their white faces, as if a chinstrap is holding on their black "caps". A giant petrel wanders through the colony in hopes of snatching an unguarded chick, but it finally gives up and flies away. Elephant seals lazily lounging on the shore almost look like beached whales. The biggest of all seals, a male could be 4.5 metres or 15 feet long, and could weigh close to four tons.

We see seals practically everywhere we go. Most are crabeater seals, not surprising since they are the most abundant seal in the world, and among the world's most plentiful large mammals. Despite its name, the crabeater feeds mostly on krill and other small fish, which it sifts through its teeth. The Weddell seal is the most southerly mammal in the world. These spotted seals live on ice that is attached to shore, and in winter spend a good deal of their time under the ice, coming up through holes to breathe.

While it's best to keep your distance from any seal, most at least appear benign or even pleasant. Except for leopard seals, which look just plain nasty. Our Zodiac passes beside an ice floe where a resting leopard seal stares menacingly at us at eye level. These giants can be up to three metres long – sleek and slender and built for speed, with an elongated reptilian-like head, powerful jaws, and an enormous mouth. Vicious predators, they are the penguin's worst nightmare, often lurking under icebergs or along shore ready to ambush any unsuspecting penguin and flail it to death.

Whale remains dot the landscape. At Mikkelsen Island we explore a vast bone yard of hundreds of whales, along with the crumbling remains of a whaling boat and various pieces of rusting equipment. For over half a century, most of the world's whaling took place in the southern oceans, where tens of thousands were killed many years. Whales hunted in this region were brought here to be processed primarily for their oil to feed the growing European market. Walking along this now isolated beach, we're dwarfed by the mostly intact skeleton of a monstrous whale. Seeing so many scattered bones is a sobering reminder of just how extensive the slaughter was.

The Antarctic Peninsula juts farther into the sea than any other part of the continent. Jagged mountains rise as high as 2,800 metres or over 9,000 feet. Technically, they are a continuation of the Andes Mountains of South America, something that both Argentina and Chile have used as a basis for claiming this part of Antarctica. To complicate things further, these areas also overlap with a claim by Britain. While various countries have made claims on Antarctica, none are internationally recognized. So far at least, the Antarctic Treaty has designated the white continent as an international zone that no one owns, and provides that Antarctica will be used for peaceful purposes only, and that no claims will be acted upon.

In many bays and inlets, gigantic glaciers line the shore. The ice sheet covering Antarctica averages about two kilometres thick, holding about 70 percent of all the fresh water in the world. The tremendous weight and pressure of the ice coupled with the forces of gravity cause glaciers to move. Their journey ends at the water's edge where monstrous chunks of ice occasionally come crashing into the sea with a thunderous roar. Icebergs of all sizes dot the bays; some melt slowly where they stand, some break into "bergy bits" or icebergs of smaller size, while others travel long distances on ocean currents. One evening at happy hour, we even have a chance to sample iceberg ice in our drinks. The irregular-shaped chunks practically explode as they contact liquid, at last releasing pressure that has accumulated for thousands of years.

Usually our trips by Zodiac take us between ship and shore, but one beautiful, almost warm afternoon, we just cruise around a maze of icebergs the size of houses, their tops a brilliant white, turning to almost unreal azure blue just below the surface. Seals bask on the lower floes while skuas and snow petrels patrol overhead. The water is dead calm. Our driver, Pablo, stops the engine and asks everyone to remain perfectly quiet. It's as if this normally cold and blustery landscape has been magically transformed, as we float in a surreal world of white and blue, surrounded by profound silence.

The next day brings a celebration. After several stops at offshore islands, the Zodiacs take us ashore for our first steps on mainland Antarctica. It's a special moment for us – we've now been to all seven continents. We watch penguins labour up the slopes taking food to their chicks, and seals lounging on shore or on ice floes. We climb to the top of a snowy ridge and gaze over spectacular ice-choked Neko Harbour, with the ship anchored in the distance.

Back on board, the chefs have decided to celebrate with a barbecue on the ship's back deck. Sitting outside in our winter jackets, we dine on barbecued steaks and chicken while looking over a breathtaking scene of icebergs, snow-capped peaks, and glaciers dripping into the sea. To top off the perfect day, we watch a colossal humpback whale breach close to the ship.

We're amazed at how different Antarctica is from the Arctic, despite the superficial similarities of ice and snow. Antarctica is a continent surrounded by ocean, while the Arctic is an ocean surrounded by land. The land mass of Antarctica is mostly covered in an ice sheet, while land ice in the Arctic is limited to certain areas, Greenland being the most obvious. There are no polar bears in Antarctica, or any land mammals for that matter, and no penguins in the Arctic. At the same latitude in the Arctic (near the Arctic Circle), plant life would be profuse. Antarctica, on the other hand, has few plants – mostly mosses, lichens, and liverworts, with some grasses, and even these are not very common. It's colder in Antarctica than the Arctic. The coldest temperature ever recorded on the planet was -89.2 degrees Celsius at the Russian Antarctic station of Vostok in 1983. For the traveller, Antarctica has one major advantage over the Arctic – no bugs.

The following day brings a visit to a raucous and smelly Adélie penguin rookery on Yalours Island. A stark black and white, with a tail a little longer than most penguins, Adélies best fit the stereotypical description of penguins as birds wearing tuxedos. Adults busily feed their mostly grown chicks by regurgitating semi-digested food. Stragglers tend tiny chicks or rest on their nests incubating eggs. One latecomer still works at building a nest which is nothing more than a shallow depression lined with pebbles. The penguin busily carries marble-sized stones, one at a time, from about 10 metres away to carefully arrange on its nest. As far as we can tell, the stones beside the nest look identical, but for whatever reason, it decides that the ones over there are much better.

Our guide takes us near a snowbank and points out an unusual phenomenon. A species of red algae has taken hold on the snow surface, turning it an almost raspberry colour. In places an entire slope carries the pinkish tinge, while in others, the red is so bright that it looks as if someone spilled a pail of paint. This type of algae often occurs in springtime when the snow melts, and takes advantage of extra nutrients in the meltwater.

Early the next morning we hear loud grinding noises and the occasional strong thunk, sure signs that we're making our way through pack ice. The ship crawls slowly along, pushing or cutting a path through heavy chunks of sea ice. It's a dramatic entrance to the famous Lemaire Channel, a narrow 11-kilometre-long passageway sandwiched between the west coast of the peninsula and islands. Said to be the most photographed part of Antarctica, we now see why. Jet-black mountains with soaring peaks rise on both sides, their cliffs either sheer vertical rock or draped with snow and glacial ice. As we nudge ice floes out of the way, penguins standing on some dive into the water, but leopard seals barely even raise their heads as we pass by.

Glimpses of research stations reveal the relatively limited human presence on the great white continent. At Mikkelsen Island, an Argentine research hut that is not currently in use sits atop a rocky ridge, looking bleak, forlorn, and forgotten even in the height of summer. What must it be like in winter? We stop at Port Lockroy, the first British scientific base in Antarctica. Closed in 1962, it has been restored and is now an historic site and museum, complete with much of the equipment used in the early days of Antarctic research. It also boasts the world's most southerly post office, mailing as many as 70,000 postcards each year to more than 100 countries. You could get home before your postcards; delivery times are usually anywhere from two to six weeks.

At Vernadsky Station, we're taken on a tour through a modern operating research station. Around a dozen or so scientists spend the winter in surprisingly comfortable digs. Originally set up by the British, the station is now run by Ukraine to study climatology, glaciology, meteorology, plus a handful of other "oligies". It was here that the hole in the ozone layer was first confirmed.

The station's other claim to fame is having the most southerly public bar in the world. It's still called the Faraday Bar, after the name of the original British station. The story goes that British carpenters at the station received a shipment of lumber intended for various repairs, but instead used most of it to build a bar, resulting in a reprimand from their superiors but a toast from their colleagues. Now it's a British pub with a Ukrainian ambiance, where vodka is the drink of choice. After the tour we retire to the lively bar to sip spicy chili pepper flavoured vodka.

Weather changes can come fast and furious. In late January, the height of the southern hemisphere summer, we can go from a pleasant 10 degrees Celsius to a full-on blizzard in a few hours.

Near the end of the trip, we stay late on deck as *Mariya Yermolova* takes us through the magnificent ice world. Snow-capped peaks rising above low scattered clouds reflect in dead calm water sparkling with icebergs and floes. The slowly setting sun dips below the horizon, bathing the sky, snow, ice, and water in soft lavender.

Next morning we wake up to a blinding snow storm. We're supposed to make one last stop before returning to Ushuaia, but when we approach Deception Island the weather goes from bad to worse, with winds too strong to negotiate the narrow passage ominously named Neptune's Bellows. The captain tries to find alternate approaches, but in each case, the storm and fierce winds make it too dangerous. Reluctantly, he turns us north to the Drake Passage and back to South America.

Leaving the islands, we catch a glimpse of another ship far in the distance. The only reason we see it at all is because we've changed our route to look for alternate landings. Cruise ships operating in these waters have coordinated their itineraries so that visits don't overlap. Though other ships may be out there, it feels like we've had this magical land at the bottom of the world all to ourselves.

It would be a toss-up to say what impresses us most – the wildlife or the stunning and austere beauty of this land of rock, ice, and water. The Antarctic experience combines these and much more, not the least of which is the uniqueness of travelling to a truly international part of the world. Even the "Drake Shake" is an essential part of the journey – a rite of passage to one of the most extraordinary places on Earth.

ABOUT THE AUTHORS

Robin and Arlene Karpan in the Athabasca Sand Dunes.

Robin and Arlene Karpan are travel writers and photographers based in Saskatoon, Saskatchewan, Canada. They are authors of several bestselling books, and their articles and photographs have appeared in over 100 publications around the world. Recognition for their work has included eight Saskatchewan Tourism Awards of Excellence, an award for photography from the North American Travel Journalists Association, and the Saskatchewan Centennial Medal. Visit *www.parklandpublishing.com* to see more of their work.